Swedish DESSERTS

80 Traditional Recipes

Recipes, text, and photos: Cecilia Vikbladh

Translated by: Stine Skarpnes Østtveit

Design and illustrations: Helena Åkesson Liedberg

Skyhorse Publishing

Skyhorse Publishing books may be purchased in bulk at special discounts
for sales promotion, corporate gifts, fundraising, or educational purposes.
Special editions can also be created to specifications. For details, contact
the Special Sales Department, Skyhorse Publishing, 307 West 36th Street,
11th Floor, New York, NY 10018 or info@skyhorsepublishing.com.

Skyhorse® and Skyhorse Publishing® are registered trademarks of
Skyhorse Publishing, Inc.®, a Delaware corporation.

Visit our website at www.skyhorsepublishing.com.

10 9 8 7 6 5 4 3 2 1

Library of Congress Cataloging-in-Publication Data is available on file.

ISBN: 978-1-61608-637-4

Printed in China

Contents

Introduction

Once you've gotten the entire stockpile of necessary ingredients home safely, there's only one thing left to do: Begin the baking. On with the apron! Then recipes for Grandma's almond mussels, Mom's saffron buns, and your favorite ginger thins are pulled out. Enjoy creating new baking traditions by trying some of the new recipes I've included in these pages.

In this book I have gathered my very best recipes. Within sections such as Classic Christmas Cookies; Winterpies, Cheesecakes, and Tarts; Cakes and Muffins; and Wheatbread and Buns you will find any tasty sweet imaginable. Whether you are interested more in traditional holiday recipes or in something more modern; I am convinced that you will find some favorites of your own in this book.

It's time to go ahead and get baking!

Good Luck!

Cecelia

Classic
Holiday Pastries

CRISPY SYRUP COOKIES

Syrup cookies, or caramel crisps, are some of the absolute best cookies in existence. They may look a little modest, but with their crispy outer crust and sticky, caramel-like core they are simply irresistible. If you want, try adding a tablespoon of cocoa or some ground almonds to the dough.

ABOUT 40 COOKIES
. . . .

200 gs / 1 ⅓ sticks butter (room temperature)
2 dl / 1 cup sugar
1 ½ dl / ⅓ cup light corn syrup
1 egg yolk
5 dl / 2 ½ cups white all-purpose flour
1 tsp vanilla extract
1 tsp baking powder

Whisk butter, sugar, corn syrup, and egg yolk together, preferably with an electric mixer.

Mix and add flour, vanilla sugar, and baking powder. Let the dough rest in the refrigerator for about 30 minutes. Set the oven to 175 C / 350 F degrees and line two baking sheets with parchment paper. Split the dough into four equal parts and roll them out on the two baking sheets so that they stretch from one end to the other lengthwise. Flatten them lightly with your hand. Bake for 15 minutes and cut into pieces while still hot. Let the cookies cool on the sheet. Store them in a tin with a lid.

Tip!

Feel free to vary the pastries by adding different flavors. You can try to add lime zest from 1 lime or 2 tbsp of cocoa to the dough. Or you may add a walnut to each pastry before you bake them. If you like cinnamon, you could sprinkle a mixture of ½ dl / ¼ cup sugar and 1 tbsp cinnamon on top before they bake.

GOLDEN JAM DREAMS

A sweet pastry like grandma used to make, something you can't be without during the holidays.

ABOUT 50 PASTRIES

200 g / 1 ⅓ sticks butter, softened
2 dl / 1 cup sugar
1 tbsp vanilla sugar

5 dl / 2 ½ cups fine white all-purpose flour

Filling:
2 dl / 1 cup raspberry jam

Set the oven to 175 C / 350 F degrees. Brown the butter carefully in a saucepan. Let it cool. Blend the sugars and butter and stir the mixture in with the flour.

Cover two baking sheets with parchment paper. Shape the dough into five long pieces and slice them each into ten smaller bits. Roll them into balls and place them on the covered baking sheets. Use your thumb to make a dent in the middle of each cookie and fill with jam. Bake for 5 to 7 minutes.

JAM STARS

Small pastries that look like pretty Christmas ornaments.

ABOUT 20 PASTRIES

1 ¼ dl / ½ cup of granulated sugar
3 ¼ dl / 1 ⅓ cups white flour
1 pinch ground cinnamon
1 pinch ground clove
1 pinch ground cardamom

200 g / 1 ⅓ sticks soft butter
100 g / 3.5 oz almonds
1 egg yolk

Filling:
1–2 dl / ½–1 cup jam or marmalade of
   your choice

Pour sugar, flour, and spices in a mixing bowl. Cut the butter into smaller pieces and blend with the spice mixture. Grind the almonds. Add the almonds and yolk to the mixture and blend it all together. Let it rest for a couple of hours in the refrigerator. Meanwhile, set the oven to 175 C / 350 F degrees.

Roll the dough out thinly. Cut into circles using a cookie cutter. Cut a pattern of your choice into the middle of half of the pastry bits. Place the pastries on a baking sheet. If you have time, you may let the baking sheet with pastries sit in the refrigerator for a while to stiffen before they bake. Cover the whole pastries with jam and add the patterned pastries on top. Bake for 15 minutes.

Tip!
Exclude the orange juice and zest.
Instead, boil the raisins in
2 dl / 1 cup glögg (the Scandinavian version of mulled wine).

SAFFRON BUNS WITH ALMOND PASTE AND ORANGE

Moist and sweet buns with a fresh taste of orange.

Dough:

150 g / 1 ¼ sticks butter

5 dl / 2 ½ cups milk

½ g / ⅓–½ tsp saffron

50 g / 2 tbsp yeast for sweet dough

½ tsp salt

1 ½ dl / ⅓ cup white all-purpose flour

13–15 dl / 5 ½–6 ½ cups wheat flour

Filling:

Grated zest and juice of 2 oranges

5 dl / 1 ½ cups raisins

100 g / 7 tbsp butter (room temperature)

½ dl / ¼ cup sugar

1–2 tbsp white all-purpose flour

150 g almond paste

Topping:

1 egg

150 g / 5 oz almond flakes

5 tbsp granulated sugar

Melt the butter in a saucepan. Add milk and saffron and let the liquid turn lukewarm. Crumble the yeast and mix it with the liquid in a bowl. Add salt, sugar, and flours. Save some of the flour for the shaping of the buns later on. Knead the dough for about 10 minutes until it's smooth. Then let it rise for about an hour or until it has doubled in size. Pour the orange juice into a small saucepan with the raisins. Let it come to a boil and then cool down.

Cover the table with flour and place the dough on top. Knead it until firm and smooth. Split the dough into two equal parts. Roll out each piece into rectangles of about 30x50 cm / 12x20 in. Blend the softened butter, grated orange zest, sugar, and almond paste (or mandelmassa). Spread the mixture over the two squares of dough. Add a layer of the boiled raisins and sprinkle the flour on top. Roll each rectangle from the long side, making sure you get it nice and tight. Slice the long rolls into pieces of about 2.5 cm / 1 in and place them in paper cups. Let them rise for an additional 30 minutes. Set the oven to 225 C / 440 F degrees. Brush the buns with the beaten egg and sprinkle almond flakes and / or granulated sugar on top. Bake for 10 to 12 minutes or until they have a nice, golden color.

OLD-FASHIONED GINGER THINS

These ginger thins taste exactly like the ones I would eat during Christmas at my grandmother's house as a child: crispy with a taste of the traditional gingerbread spices and a refreshing touch of lemon. The dough is smooth and easy to work with, and it is perfect for making into shapes and figures.

20–30 THINS

2 tbsp ground cinnamon
1 tbsp ground ginger
1 tbsp ground cloves
1 tbsp ground cardamom
1 tsp salt
1 tbsp baking soda
300g / 2 ½ sticks butter (room temperature)
2 ½ dl / 1 ¼ cups sugar
2 dl / 1 cup brown sugar

1 egg
Finely grated zest of 1 lemon
3 dl / 1 ½ cups light corn syrup
3 dl / 1 ½ cups heavy whipping cream
1.7–1.8 dl / ⅓ cup white all-purpose
    flour

Frosting:
150 g / 5 oz powdered sugar
1 tbsp lemon juice
1 egg white

Whisk together cinnamon, ginger, cloves, cardamom, salt, and baking soda. Mix butter, sugar, brown sugar, egg, and the spice mix into a dough. Add the lemon zest, syrup, cream, and flour and work it into an even dough. Let it sit in the refrigerator overnight.

Preheat the oven to 175 C / 350 F degrees. Knead the dough until it is soft and smooth. Split it into smaller parts. Spread a layer of flour on the table. Roll the dough out as thin as you can. Occasionally lift the dough up off the table, add some more flour, and continue so as to keep it from sticking. Create shapes with the help of cookie cutters. Place them on parchment paper on a baking sheet. Bake for 8 to 10 minutes. Whisk the ingredients for the frosting together. If you end up not using all of the frosting for this one batch, you can easily keep it in the refrigerator covered with plastic wrap.

SAFFRON BUNS

Despite all the fantastic new additions to the cake family, I still can't resist saving some pages for the incredibly flavorful saffron buns. You bake this particular variety with two separate kinds of dough. They're a bit more time consuming than the "regular" saffron buns, but it is worth it. More moist or airy saffron buns are nearly impossible to come by.

60–70 SAFFRON BUNS

Dough 1:
5 dl / 2 ½ cups milk
75 g / 3 ½ tbsp yeast
1 dl / ½ cup sugar
12 dl / 6 cups white all-purpose flour
1 g (2 packets) / 1 ½ tsp saffron

Dough 2:
4 dl / 2 cups milk
2 dl / 1 cup sugar
300 g / 2 ½ sticks butter
    (room temperature)
6 egg yolks
1 pinch of salt
Egg to brush the top
Raisins and granulated sugar

Warm the milk for the first dough until lukewarm and pour it into a bowl or food processor. Add the yeast, sugar, flour, and saffron. Knead the dough for at least 5 minutes and then let it rise for an hour.

Warm the milk for the second dough until lukewarm. Pour milk, sugar, butter, yolks, salt, and flour into the bowl with the first dough. Work it for about 10 minutes, until it's one smooth dough. Let it rise for 90 minutes.

Place the dough on a table sprinkled with flour and shape the saffron buns (as pictured). Place them on baking sheets lined with parchment paper. Set the oven to 175 C / 350 F degrees. Let the buns rise for an additional 30 minutes. Brush them with beaten egg and decorate with raisins and granulated sugar. Bake for 8 to 12 minutes, depending on how large you made the buns.

PANFORTE FROM SIENNA

This recipe stems from the Middle Ages in Italy. You may make this cake year-round, but it is first and foremost prepared during the holidays. It is often sold as beautifully wrapped, small-portioned cakes. Panforte means "strong bread," which refers to the fact that this cake contains spices, such as white pepper and ginger. The ingredients of panforte vary greatly from recipe to recipe. This variety includes generous amounts of chocolate, nuts, and honey and tastes heavenly.

ABOUT 50 SMALL PIECES

200 g / 7 oz dried figs

200 g / 7 oz dried apricots

100 g / 3.5 oz pickled ginger

200 g / 7 oz dark chocolate

500 g / 1 ½ cups honey

250 g / 1 ⅛ cups sugar

500 g / 1 lb nuts of your choice
    (for instance, walnuts or almonds)

100 g / ½ cup raisins

250 g / 2 cups white all-purpose
    flour

100 g / ⅞ cups cocoa

1 tbsp ground cinnamon

1 tbsp ground ginger

1 tsp ground white pepper

2 tbsp powdered sugar for decorating

Chop figs, apricots, and ginger. Break the chocolate into smaller pieces and let it melt slowly in the microwave or in a double boiler on the stove. Make sure that no water spills on the chocolate. Let the chocolate cool. Set the oven to 150 C / 300 F degrees. Lightly roast the nuts. Mix honey and sugar in a pan with a thick bottom. First, melt it slowly on the stove and then let it come to a boil. Do a marble test to see if the sugar mixture is done: Pour a teaspoon of the sugar mixture into a glass of cold water. When you can shape a marble out of the syrup, it is ready. Add the melted chocolate to the sugar and mix well. Pour all of it into a large bowl. Mix in the rest of the ingredients and stir the heavy blend as best as you can. Line a springform pan, about 26 cm / 10 in. in diameter, with parchment paper. Scoop the mixture into the pan and bake for 30 minutes. Let the cake cool completely before you cut it. Top with powdered sugar before you serve.

Tip!

When you prepare this kind of pastry or sweet it's very helpful to have a thermometer available. The sugar mixture is usually done at 112–115 C / 233–240 F degrees; at this point you can shape it into a soft marble (this is called a soft marble test). We call it a hard marble test when the marble keeps its shape even under slight pressure.

Tip!

You can easily end up with imperfections along the edges when you glue the house together using sugar—simply hide these with frosting. Gingerbread houses should not be rolled out too thin; about 3 mm is perfect for this. They need to bake for a long time, but should not be burnt; this will ruin the overall esthetic. If you bake them too little, however, the parts will be too soft and the house will crumble.

GINGERBREAD HOUSE

Finally it's standing there, proud and decorated. Thanks to our neighbors' kids, the house looks great. Make sure to set aside enough time for the construction of the gingerbread house; this is not something that should be done under time pressure. This recipe makes more than enough dough, which is good because you may have to remake a section should you make a mistake. Decorate with frosting before you construct the house.

Dough:

5 ½ dl / 1 ⅓ cups sugar

5 dl / 1 ½ cups dark corn syrup or
   light molasses

200 g / 1 ⅓ sticks butter

16–17 dl / 6–7 cups white
   all-purpose flour

1 ½ tbsp baking soda

2 tsp ground ginger

2 tsp ground cloves

2 tsp ground cinnamon

1 ½ dl / ⅓ cup water

Frosting:

1 egg white

4 dl / 2 cups powdered sugar

½ tsp vinegar

Snow:

5 dl / 1 ½ cups powdered sugar

For decorating:

Gelatin sheets for windows, carton to
   make the templates, candies, cake
   decorations, and other decorations
   of choice

Boil sugar, syrup, and butter in a pot with a thick bottom. Mix the dry ingredients with the water in a food processor or by hand. Pour the warm sugar blend into the mix. Knead until the dough is even. Cover with plastic wrap and let it sit overnight at room temperature.

Knead and roll out the dough on a table lightly powdered with flour. Carve out the shapes for the house by tracing the paper templates with a knife. (See specifics for template on p. 123). Bake at 175–200 C / 350–390 F degrees. Upon removing them from the oven, directly place the templates on top and carve / adjust as needed. Then let the pieces cool down on the sheet. Whisk the egg whites well and add the other ingredients for the frosting. Add water if it is too gluey, but it is not supposed to be completely fluid.

Melt the powdered sugar for the frosting in a frying pan on medium heat. Then lower the heat so that the sugar is no longer boiling but will keep the same consistency. Place the warm sugar in a pastry bag and use the frosting to glue the house together. (A plastic bag with the tip cut off also works.) Cut pieces of gelatin sheets for the windows and glue them on with frosting.

ALMOND MUSSELS

*It can be somewhat tricky to bake almond mussels. It is important that
you butter the cake forms well; if not, the cakes might stick. (A Swedish
almond mussel pan is traditionally used, but a small bundt cake pan can
work just as well.) Squeeze the forms between the thumb and the index
finger and they usually let go of the cakes. If not, thump the cake forms
lightly on the table. It is preferable to grind the almonds in a nut grinder.
Fill the mussels with lightly whipped heavy cream and a tasty jam right
before serving.*

ABOUT 40 MUSSELS

1 ½ dl / ⅓ cup sweet almonds
4 bitter almonds
200 g / 1 ⅓ sticks butter (room temperature)
1 ½ dl / ⅓ cup sugar
4–5 dl / 2– 2 ½ cups white all-purpose flour
1 egg

Shell the almonds. Dry them well and grind them in a nut grinder. Whisk butter and sugar until light and creamy. Add the flour and the ground almonds
to the mixture. Add the egg. Work the dough. Let it rest in a cold place for 20
minutes. Butter the cake forms. Set the oven to 175–200 C / 350–390 F degrees. Split the dough into 40 pieces and place the pieces in the cake forms.
You may use your fingers, but dip them in flour first. Bake for 7 minutes. Let
cool for a while and then move onto a cooling rack to let cool completely.

Tip!

You will get a different and very tasty variety of
almond mussels if you add ½ dl / ¼ cup of cocoa to
the dough. Serve with 2 dl / 1 cup whipped cream
flavored with 2–3 tbsp port wine. Scoop cream onto
the chocolate mussels and stick a fig in the cream.

16

Tip!

· Whisk eggs and sugar for at least 5 minutes.
· Brush cold water on the parchment paper so it won't stick to the cake.
· Roll the cake together as quickly as possible so that it doesn't dry or crack.
· If there's butter or cream in the filling, the cake has to cool down before you add the filling.

SAFFRON ROLL CAKE WITH LEMON CURD

Roll cakes are one of the easiest pastries to bake. Not to mention the fact that you can vary the taste of both the dough and the filling. This simple roll cake is especially good with a filling of lemon curd and cream.

ABOUT 10 PIECES

5 large eggs
2 dl / 1 cup sugar
1 tbsp water
½ g (1 packet) / ⅓–½ tsp saffron
2 dl / 1 cup white all-purpose flour
2 tsp baking powder
Finely grated zest of 1 lemon

Filling:
2 dl / 1 cup heavy whipping cream
2 dl / 1 cup lemon curd
2–3 tbsp sugar for the paper

Set the oven to 250 C / 480 F degrees. Whisk the eggs and sugar until white and fluffy. Bring the water to a boil and add the saffron. Let it sit for 5 minutes. Pour the saffron water in with the egg mixture. Blend the flour and baking powder and add that to the mixture as well. Add half of the lemon zest. Line a baking pan with parchment paper and spread the mixture on top. Leave a small border of about 2 cm / 1 in along the edges. Bake for about 5 minutes.

Place a piece of parchment paper on the table. Sprinkle the sugar and the rest of the lemon zest on the paper. Place the cake on the paper and then pull the paper out from under the cake. Let the cake cool down. Whip the cream and blend it with the lemon curd. Cover the cake with the filling and roll it up. Let the roll sit for a while, with the seam facing down, before you cut it into pieces.

FRUITCAKE WITH AMARETTO AND SNOW FROSTING

People have been baking this fruitcake for hundreds of years in a variety of ways. The Amaretto in this recipe gives it a taste of Italy. Apricots, lemon zest, raisins, and pickled orange peels also contribute to the fresh taste and juicy consistency. The cake will keep for a couple of weeks if you keep it well wrapped in the fridge.

16–18 PIECES

300 g / 10 oz dried apricots
2 dl / 1 cup Amaretto (or other liqueur)
1 vanilla bean
3 dl / 1 ½ cups sugar
250 g / 2 sticks butter (room temperature)
4 eggs
Juice and grated zest of 1 lemon
100 g / ½ cup raisins
100 g / 3.5 oz finely chopped pickled orange peels
4 dl / 2 cups white all-purpose flour

Frosting:
2 egg whites
5–6 dl / 2 ½–3 cups powdered sugar
1 tsp lemon juice
1 tsp gelatin

Finely chop the apricots so that the bits are the approximate size of raisins. Soak them in the liqueur for at least two hours. Set the oven to 175 C / 350 F degrees. Split the vanilla bean in two lengthwise and scrape the seeds into a mixer. Add the sugar and mix well. Scoop the butter into the bowl and blend until it's an even batter. Pour the batter into a bowl and stir the eggs into the batter one at a time. Then add the liquid from the apricot blend. Mix apricots, lemon juice and zest, raisins, and pickled orange peel with the flour. Add the mix to the batter. Butter and flour a springform pan of about 24 cm / 9 ½ in. in diameter. Pour the batter into the form and bake for 75 to 90 minutes, depending on the size of the form. Test with a toothpick to see if the cake is ready. Let it cool.

Beat the egg whites until stiff and white. Whisk some powdered sugar in with the eggs and add the lemon juice and gelatin. Stir in the rest of the powdered sugar in increments. Cover the cake with a thick layer of the frosting. Decorate with sprinkles if you like.

CRISPY SAFFRON CRUSTS

Delightful, golden crusts that melt in your mouth. They contain an abun-dance of butter that makes them tender and crispy.

. . . .

4 tbsp water

1 g (2 packets) / 1.5 tsp saffron

200 g / 1 cup butter, room temperature

2 dl / 1 cup raw cane sugar

4 eggs

1 tsp salt

10 dl / 5 cups white all-purpose flour

1 egg for brushing the top

Let the water come to a boil. Add the saffron. Whisk butter and sugar until white and fluffy. Add the saffron water. Stir in one egg at a time. Add salt. Stir the flour in with the batter and stir into a dough that's easy to shape. Let the dough rest in the refrigerator for an hour. Set the oven to 200 C / 390 F degrees.

Place the dough on the table. Shape it into four long parts, about 1 cm / ½ in. high. Place them on a baking sheet lined with parchment paper and brush with the egg. Bake for 10 to 12 minutes. Remove the pieces and cut them into diagonal sections. Raise the heat of the oven to 250 C / 480 F degrees. Place the crusts on their sides on the sheet. Roast them until they get a nice color, about 5 minutes, keeping a close eye on them so that they do not burn. Lower the temperature to 50 C / 120 F and let the crusts dry for a couple of hours. Have the oven door slightly ajar, with a gap of about 3 cm / 1 in.; you can place a tree spoon or similar in the door to help keep the gap open. Store the crusts in a closed tin at room temperature.

WHEY BUTTERSCOTCH

The world's best butterscotch! Whey butter is excellent for candies as it has a hint of a caramel taste. This butterscotch is a teensy bit salty, which makes it irresistible.

ABOUT 50 BUTTERSCOTCH PIECES

½ dl / ¼ cup sweet almonds
1 ½ dl / ⅓ cup light corn syrup
1 ½ tbsp butter
1 dl / ½ cup heavy whipping cream
1 dl / ½ cup sugar
1 dl / ½ cup whey butter

Blanch, shell, and finely chop the almonds. Mix all of the ingredients, except the almonds, in a pan. Let it come to a boil and do a soft marble test continually. If you have a thermometer, the butterscotch is ready at 125 C / 260 F degrees. Add the almonds and pour the blend into butterscotch forms. Let it stiffen.

Tip!

Here are a few suggestions for different butterscotch flavors: Add one teaspoon gingerbread spices, vanilla sugar, ground ginger, cocoa, or coffee to the batter. Crushed peppermint sticks instead of almonds will give a fresh taste of mint. A little bit of nicely grated lemon zest in the batter will also add great taste.

CHOCOLATE FUDGE WITH
MARSHMALLOWS AND NUTS

Supertasty, soft, and chewy sweets with a hint of walnuts. Although cal-
led fudge today, these Swedish treats originally inspired the American
version of fudge. The difference between this chocolate marble fudge
confection we'll make here and American fudge is that this one is softer,
drier, and melts in your mouth. Feel free to flavor the batter with whis-
key, peanut butter, peanuts, or other nut varieties.

ABOUT 40 BITES
. . . .

1 ½ dl / ⅓ cup milk
4 dl / 2 cups sugar
1 ¼ dl / ⅔ cup brown sugar
150 g / 1 ¼ sticks butter

100 g / 3.5 oz dark chocolate
    (60–70 percent)
½ dl / ¼ cup honey
150 g / 5 oz marshmallows (mini or
    chopped regulars)
100 g / 3.5 oz walnuts

Warm the milk, sugar, and brown sugar in a saucepan. Stir until the sugar
is completely melted. Add the butter, chocolate, and honey while still stirring continuously. Let it boil under a lid for about two minutes. Remove the
lid and continue boiling. Do a marble test now and then to see if it is ready.
You should be able to shape a soft marble, which takes about 12 minutes.
The time is dependent upon how thick the bottom of your saucepan is.
Make sure that the batter doesn't cook for too long in your saucepan. Take
care that the mixture does not boil.

Remove the saucepan from the stove and place it in a water bath. Stir the batter until it's creamy and somewhat lighter. Add the nuts and marshmallows. Butter a baking pan, about 20x20 cm / 8x8 in, and line it with parchment paper. Pour the batter into the pan and let it cool. Let it stiffen completely in the refrigerator and then take it out and cut it into pieces.

DARK CHOCOLATE SWEETS

A very simple chocolate recipe. The combination of chocolate, nuts, and dried fruit is always a sure success.

200 g / 7 oz mixed nuts
300 g / 10 oz dark chocolate (70 percent)
½ tsp sesame seeds
¼ tsp chili powder
½ tsp salt

Chop the nuts and spread them out in cookie pans or on a sheet of parchment paper on a baking pan. Melt the chocolate and scoop it over the nuts. When the chocolate has started to stiffen it is time to sprinkle the rest of the ingredients on top. Keep the chocolate in the refrigerator until it's completely cool. Break it into pieces to serve.

CHOCOLATE AND FIG GLOBES

Wonderful fig globes with almonds and coconut. Store them in a container with a tight lid or in a plastic bag in the refrigerator. The globes will keep for multiple weeks in the refrigerator.

ABOUT 30 BALLS

250 g / 8 oz or about 8 soft dried figs

100 g / 1 cup almonds

3 tbsp cocoa

50 g / 3.5 tbsp butter

2 dl / 1 cup coconut flakes

> ## Tip!
> Add 2 tbsp of light rum. The rum taste goes great with both chocolate and almonds.

Cut off the hard stem of the figs. Chop the almonds and figs into smaller pieces. Blend the figs, almonds, and cocoa in a food processor. Add the butter and mix for a while longer. Roll small balls of the batter. Pour coconut flakes on a plate and roll the balls in it. Keep the finished globes in the refrigerator.

Cookies

BRUSSELS COOKIES

Well-known crunchy cookies with a vanilla scent. These are even more delicious if you make your own vanilla sugar, but it works just fine with store-bought vanilla sugar as well. This is a good base cookie dough, and if you want you can flavor the batter with a few tablespoons of cocoa for tasty chocolate cookies. In that case, brush the cookies with egg and decorate with almonds or granulated sugar.

ABOUT 60 COOKIES
. . . .

½ dl / ¼ cup sugar, and a few drops of red
    food coloring, or colored sugar
375 g / 3 ⅓ sticks butter
2 dl / 1 cup powdered sugar
1 tbsp vanilla sugar, homemade if possible
8–9 dl / 4–4 ½ cups white all-purpose flour

Start by mixing one to two drops of the food coloring with the sugar. Place the colored sugar onto a plate so that it dries. Then place all of the ingredients in a bowl and mix into a batter. Split the dough into three pieces and roll into logs 3–4 cm / 1–1 ½ in. in diameter. Pour the colored sugar on the table and roll the cookie dough in it. Wrap them in plastic wrap and let them cool in the refrigerator for an hour. Set the oven to 175 C / 350 F degrees. Slice 1 cm / ½ in. pieces of the dough. Then place the pieces on a lined baking sheet. Bake till they're lightly golden, about 12 minutes.

From the left: Crunchy lemon and poppy seed cookies, peanut and marmalade cookies, chocolate cookies with pistachio nuts, Brussels cakes, and crispy caramel cookies.

Homemade Vanilla Sugar

Split a vanilla bean down the middle and scrape the seeds into a bowl with 4 dl / 2 cups of sugar. Then chop the bean into small pieces and mix it all in a food processor until it's evenly distributed. Use a sifter to remove the larger pieces. If you only use a couple of tablespoons of vanilla sugar at a time you can keep adding on sugar for the first couple of uses. This is because it will still be developing its flavor for a period of time. There is also a cheaper version of this that works well: The next time you use vanilla seeds, save the stick and run it in a mixer with 3 dl / 1 ½ cups sugar. Then remove the large pieces with a sifter.

CHOCOLATE COOKIES WITH PISTACHIO NUTS

These small cookies are as pretty as pralines. With a rich chocolate flavor and crunchy nuts, this is another cookie that will be snatched from the coffee table before you have time to wink. If you want, make a double batch.

ABOUT 40 COOKIES

3 dl / 1 ½ cups bitter almonds
200 g / 1 ⅓ sticks refrigerated butter
1 dl / ½ cup sugar
5 ½ dl / 2 ⅓ cups white all-purpose flour
1 dl / ½ cup cocoa
1 egg
½ dl / ¼ cup chopped pistachios
2 tbsp granulated sugar

Finely grind the bitter almonds. Cut the butter into smaller pieces and mix with bitter almonds, sugar, flour, and cocoa. Work the dough by hand or use a food processor. Split the dough into four equal pieces and roll logs of about 3–4 cm / 1–2 in. diameter. Wrap them in plastic wrap and place them in the fridge for about an hour. Set the oven to 200 C / 390 F degrees. Cut each roll into ten slices and place the cookies on a lined baking sheet.

Brush the cookies with a beaten egg. Sprinkle chopped pistachios and granulated sugar on top. Bake for 10 minutes. Let them cool for a while on the sheet before you move them onto a cooling rack. (See picture p. 31.)

CRISPY CARAMEL COOKIES

Cookies with a candy feel that melt in your mouth. The brown sugar accentuates the caramel taste and gives the cookie a smooth and enjoyable taste.

ABOUT 20 COOKIES

100 g / 3.5 oz sweet almonds
100 g / 7 tbsp butter (room temperature)
½ dl / ¼ cup sugar
1 dl / ½ cup light brown sugar
1 pinch of salt
2 ½ dl / 1 ¼ cups white all-purpose flour
½ tsp baking powder
200 g / 7 oz crushed hard caramel (use the Scandinavian candy
    Daim or a Hesey Skor bar if possible)
1 egg

Set the oven to 225 C / 440 F degrees. Chop the almonds. Stir the butter in with the almonds, sugar, brown sugar, salt, flour, baking powder, and caramel bits. Lastly, add the egg.

Shape the lump of dough and roll it into a log of about 8 cm / 3 in. diameter. Wrap it in plastic wrap and let it rest in the fridge for about 30 minutes. Slice 1 cm / ½ in. pieces and place them on a lined baking sheet. Bake in the oven for 8 to 10 minutes or until the cookies' edges are light brown. (See picture p. 31.)

> ## Tip!
> Instead of crushed hard caramels you can
> flavor the dough with 125 g / 4.5 oz of hard
> peppermint candies or candy canes.

CRUNCHY LEMON AND
POPPY SEED COOKIES

Flavorful shortbread cookies that taste the absolute best served with glögg (mulled wine) or a cup of tea. The combination of lemon and nutty poppy seeds is often found in England and the United States.

ABOUT 25 COOKIES

3 dl / 1 ½ cups white all-purpose flour

A pinch of salt

1 dl / ½ cup powdered sugar

1 dl / ½ cup raw cane sugar

Finely grated zest of 1 lemon

2 tsp poppy seeds

125 g / 1 stick cold butter

1 egg

Mix flour, raw cane sugar, salt, lemon zest, and poppy seeds in a food processor. Dice the butter and add to the mixture while the mixer is still running. Lastly, add the egg. Turn the machine off when the dough has formed into a lump. Shape the dough into a loaf, about 8 cm / 3 in. in diameter and wrap it in plastic wrap. Let it sit in the refrigerator until it is completely stiff, at least two hours. Set the oven to 200 C / 390 F degrees. Cut ½ cm / ¼ in. slices and place them on a lined baking sheet. Bake for 10 to 12 minutes or until the cookies' edges have a slight color. Move the cookies onto a cooling rack and let them cool. Dust with powdered sugar before serving. (See picture p. 31.)

Tip!
You can save the loaf of dough in the fridge for up to a week. If you don't use all the dough at once you may bake more later.

PEANUT AND MARMALADE COOKIES

American as it is, this is a refined version of the "peanut butter and jelly sandwich." A super tasty cookie that even the gluten intolerant may feast on. The cookies are very crispy, and with the accompanying marmalade they taste heavenly.

12 DOUBLE COOKIES

275 g / 9.5 oz chunky peanut butter

2 dl / 1 cup cane sugar

1 large egg

2 tsp vanilla sugar

About 1 dl / ½ cup jam, marmalade, or jelly

Set the oven to 200 C / 390 F degrees. Whisk the peanut butter and cane sugar together. Beat the egg separately in a cup. Add the vanilla sugar and beaten egg. Shape the quite-firm batter into 24 marbles. Place the marbles on a baking sheet lined with buttered parchment paper. Flatten them with a fork. Bake the cookies for 15 minutes or until they are slightly brown at the edges. Let them cool a bit on the baking sheet before you move them onto a wire rack to let them cool completely. Stack the cookies in two's, like a sandwich, with jam, marmalade, or jelly in between.

ALFAJORES DE DULCE DE LECHE

*From Argentina with love come these crisp delicious cookies. They are fil-
led with a thick and creamy caramel filling (also known as dulce de leche)
and later rolled in grated coconut. You can find this cookie in certain parts
of Spain, but first and foremost in the South American countries. It is
perceived as the national cookie of Argentina, despite the fact that it has
roots in the Middle East. There, this cookie is eaten daily—for breakfast,
dessert, a snack, basically any occasion imaginable.*

ABOUT 20 SANDWICHED COOKIES

1 can of sweetened condensed milk
2 dl / 1 cup sugar
250 g / 2 sticks butter
5 egg yolks
Finely grated zest of 1 lemon
1 tbsp lemon juice

1 tsp baking soda
2 tsp baking powder
1 tsp vanilla extract
4 dl / 2 cups white
5 ½ dl / 1 ⅓ cups corn starch
2 dl / 1 cup grated coconut

Begin by making the caramel cream. Simmer the can of condensed milk in
a saucepan with water for 4 to 5 hours. It is very important that the can is
covered by water at all times. If not, the can may explode. Afterwards, soak
the can in cold water and let it cool completely before you open it. The milk
will have transformed into a smooth, creamy, caramel colored sauce, dulce
de leche!

Set the oven to 225 C / 440 F degrees. Whisk sugar and butter into a
batter. Add the yolks, vanilla extract, lemon zest, and juice and blend well.
Mix baking soda, baking powder, flour, and cornstarch and stir into the batter as well.

Place the dough on a floured table and roll it out to about ½ cm / ¼ in
thickness. Cut out about 40 cookies of about 6 cm / 2 ⅓ in. diameter by
using a glass or a cookie cutter. Bake for 5 to 7 minutes or until the cookies
are golden brown. Let the cookies cool. Turn half of the cookies bottom
side up and spread each with about 1 tbsp of dulce de leche. Top with
remaining cookies, bottom side down. Place coconut in a shallow bowl.
Gently squeeze each sandwich until filling begins to show at edges, then
roll edges in coconut.

Tip!

It is also possible to cook the caramel sauce by punching a teeny hole on the top of the can of condensed milk, and always keeping the water below the hole. However, this takes even longer. It is the high pressure inside of the can that makes it go faster when it is completely covered by water.

MACARONS WITH THREE FILLINGS

Whether they are candy or cookies is hard to determine, but there's little doubt that these are excellent on the dessert table, accompanied by butter marbles and almond butterscotch. It is a bit tricky and time consuming to make macarons, but it's worth every minute. The fillings should sit for a while in the fridge so that they obtain a spreadable consistency, but make sure that they do not harden completely. The filling varieties below are enough for one batch of macarons.

ABOUT 20 MACARONS
. . . .

Macaron crust:
250 g / 9 oz almond paste
1 dl / ½ cup granulated sugar
1 egg white

White chocolate filling:
300 g / 10 oz white chocolate

2 dl / 1 cup heavy whipping cream
50 g / 3 ½ tbsp butter
½ dl / ¼ cup cognac

Glaze shell:
200 g / 7 oz white chocolate
1 tbsp corn oil

Set the oven to 175 C / 350 F degrees. Grate the almond paste and add the sugar. Add the egg white and stir until you have an even mixture. Scoop the batter onto a lined baking sheet in small rounds the size of a silver dollar. Alternatively, scoop the batter into a pastry bag and squeeze it out. Bake the crusts for about 10 minutes or until they are golden brown. Let them cool and then remove them from the parchment paper.

Roughly chop 300 g / 10 oz white chocolate. Melt on low heat in a saucepan with a thick bottom. Add cream and butter while stirring. Lastly, add the cognac. Whip the cream until it's cool and feels fluffy. Turn the cakes upside-down and place them on parchment paper. Add a rounded dab of filling on each crust and let them rest in the refrigerator for at least an hour. If possible, you may place them in the freezer for a little while before you add the glaze shell. Melt the chocolate for the shell in a saucepan and stir in the oil. Dip the cream tops quickly in the chocolate. Keep the macarons cold.

Dark chocolate buttercream:
1 egg white from a large egg
1 tsp lemon juice
1 ½ dl / ⅓ cup sugar
250 g / 2 sticks unsalted butter (room temperature)
125 g / 4.5 oz dark chocolate (70 percent)
400 g / 14 oz dark chocolate

Mix the egg white, lemon juice, and sugar in a saucepan with a thick bottom. Warm the ingredients on low heat before you start whisking them together. Measure the temperature with a digital thermometer and remove the blend when it has reached 60 C / 140 F degrees. Keep whisking until the batter has cooled. Add the butter in pieces and whisk for another 10 minutes. Warm 125 g / 4.5 oz chocolate on low heat and let it melt. Pour the buttercream into the chocolate in a thin stream, stirring the whole time. Add a rounded dab of the cream onto the macaron crusts and put them in the fridge so that they harden. Melt the rest of the chocolate. Dip the chocolate cream tops quickly in the melted chocolate. Store cold.

Lemon filling:
³ / ⁴dl / 5 tbsp lemon juice
1 / 3 dl / 5 tsp sugar
3 egg yolks
Grated zest of 2 lemons
150 g / 1 ¼ stick butter (room temperature)
150 g / 5 oz white chocolate

Boil sifted lemon juice and sugar into thick syrup. Take one teaspoon of the blend and carefully blow on it. Dip the tip of your thumb and index finger in the liquid. Press the fingers together and then pull apart. When you see a small thread between your fingers while doing this, the syrup is ready. Beat the egg yolks in a bowl with an electric mixer on medium speed while you slowly add warm, not hot, sugar syrup and lemon zest. Let it cool. Stir in the butter one piece at a time. Add rounded dabs of the filling to the macaron crusts and set them in the freezer for an hour. Melt the white chocolate and then dip the lemon cream tops quickly in the chocolate. Store cold.

COOKIE WITH WHITE CHOCOLATE AND MACADAMIA NUTS

The combination of white chocolate and macadamia nuts is pure perfection. Be alert when you make this because white chocolate burns very easily.

ABOUT 20 COOKIES

150 g / 5 oz white chocolate
100 g / 3.5 oz salted macadamia nuts
175 g / 1 ½ sticks butter (room temperature)
1 dl / ½ cup cane sugar

3 dl / 1 ½ cups white all-purpose flour
1 tsp baking powder
1 pinch of salt
1 egg
1 tsp vanilla sugar

Set the oven to 200 C / 390 F degrees. Roughly chop the chocolate and nuts. Stir or whisk butter and sugar into a fluffy batter. Mix flour, baking powder, and salt together. Beat the egg and stir it in with the butter batter. Add the mixture of dry ingredients. Lastly, stir in the vanilla sugar, chocolate, and nuts. Place spoonfuls of the batter on a lined baking sheet and flatten them a bit. Bake for 10 to 15 minutes. The cookies are done when the edges are golden brown.

CHOCOLATE CHIP COOKIES

Real chocolate cookies with bountiful taste. Feel free to test this recipe with different kinds of sugars and chocolates. Both dark and white chocolate are great for this. You can even vary it with other flavors, such as cinnamon, coconut, lemon, or peanuts.

ABOUT 20 LARGE COOKIES

150 g / 1 ¼ sticks butter
3 dl / 1 ½ cups dark brown sugar
2 dl / 1 cup cane sugar
1 tbsp vanilla sugar
2 eggs
7 dl / 3 ½ cups oats
3 dl / 1 ½ cups wheat flour
1 pinch of salt
1 tsp baking powder
200 g / 7 oz milk chocolate
50 g / 1.7 oz hazelnuts or walnuts

Set the oven to 180 C / 360 F degrees. Melt the butter in a saucepan and stir in the three sugars. Stir until it has obtained a creamy texture. Pour the butter blend into a bowl. Beat the eggs lightly and mix it in with the butter blend. Mix oats, flour, salt, and baking powder in a separate bowl. Add the dry ingredients to the batter a little at a time. It is easiest to use a wooden spoon to stir this. Roughly chop the chocolate and nuts and add them to the batter. Shape golf ball–sized spheres and flatten them on parchment paper. Bake on a baking sheet for 8 to 10 minutes.

CHOCOLATE AND HAZELNUT STARS

These cookies are just as beautiful as holiday decorations. Use home-made chocolate cream or Nutella as a filling. If you have time and you are looking for a fresher taste, you must try the delicious passion fruit curd on p. 110.

ABOUT 20 COOKIES

125 g / 4.5 oz hazelnuts
125 g / 4.5 oz almonds
4 dl / 2 cups powdered sugar
1 tsp vanilla sugar
1 egg
Chocolate cream (recipe p. 109)

Roast the nuts in a dry frying pan until they start browning. Place the nuts on a kitchen towel. Fold the towel together and rub the nuts against each other and the cloth. Open the cloth and remove the shells of the nuts.

Scald and peel the almonds. Grind the shelled almonds and hazelnuts in a nut grinder or food processor. They have to be ground into fine flour; if not, the cookies won't obtain the right texture. Blend the sugar, vanilla sugar, and the egg in the food processor with the nut meal. Let it mix into a dough. Cover in plastic wrap and let it sit in the refrigerator for about two hours.

Set the oven to 200 C / 390 F degrees. Place the dough on a baking sheet covered with a thin layer of powdered sugar. Roll out the dough thinly. Cut about 40 star shapes using a cookie cutter. Gather the remaining dough and repeat the process until you've cut as many stars as possible. Bake for 8 to 10 minutes or until the edges are a bit brown. Let it cool on a cooling rack.

Spread the chocolate cream on half of the cookies and cover with the other half. Sprinkle some powdered sugar on top before serving.

SICILIAN ALMOND COOKIES

Pastries and desserts from Sicily are often inspired by the North African food culture. Almonds, other nuts, and dried fruits are common ingredients. Try these lovely cookies with a cup of espresso.

ABOUT 40 COOKIES

600 g / 1.3 lbs sweet almonds
4 dl / 2 cups sugar
4 egg whites (large eggs)
½ dl / ¼ cup Amaretto (almond liqueur)
2 drops of almond extract
1 dl / ½ cup powdered sugar

Scald and shell the almonds. Dry them with a kitchen towel or broil them in the oven at about 100 C / 210 F degrees for a short while. They are absolutely not supposed to be roasted, just dried. Grind the almonds in a nut grinder or a food processor. Be attentive and make sure that there are no large bits left. Pour the sugar into the food processor and mix with the almonds into a fine meal. Move the almond and sugar mixture to a bowl and stir in the egg white, liqueur, and almond extract. Stir into an even extract. Set the oven to 175 C / 350 F degrees.

Shape 40 balls the size of a walnut. Carefully roll them in powdered sugar and shape a round tip. Place the cakes on two buttered pieces of parchment paper. Bake in the middle of the oven for 15 minutes. Roll the cookies in plenty of powdered sugar and let them cool. Store them in a cool and dry place.

BUTTERSCOTCH COOKIES WITH
CRANBERRY DIP

These butterscotch cookies with raisins, nuts, and chocolate are delicious just as they are. But you have to test them with the cranberry cream. Unbeatable. The cookies bake quickly, but they will be at their absolute best if the dough rests over night.

ABOUT 70 COOKIES
. . . .
300 g / 2 ½ sticks butter
   (room temperature)
5 dl / 2 ½ cups sugar
2 dl / 1 cup light corn syrup
2 eggs
250 g / 9 oz raisins
100 g / 3.5 oz hazelnuts
150 g / 5 oz dark chocolate (70 percent)

12 dl / 6 cups white all-purpose flour
1 ½ tbsp baking soda

Cranberry dip:
200 g / 7 oz cream cheese (for example,
   Philadelphia cream cheese)
200 g / 7 oz frozen or fresh
   cranberries
1 tbsp fruit punch
½ dl / ¼ cup of honey
2 dl / 1 cup crème fraiche

Whisk a batter out of the sugar and butter. Add the corn syrup, eggs, raisins, roughly chopped nuts, and roughly chopped chocolate. Mix the flour and baking soda together and add it to the batter. Let the dough rest overnight.

Set the oven to 175 C / 350 F degrees. Split the dough into eight parts. Roll a log from each piece, with about a 3 cm / 1 in. diameter. Place the rolls in pairs on a cooking sheet. Flatten them a bit. Bake for 12 to 15 minutes or until they are light brown. Cut into diagonal slices while they are still on the sheet. Let them cool.

Mix cream cheese, cranberries, and honey in a food processor. Stir the punch and crème fraiche together in a separate bowl. Lastly, slowly mix the punch mixture in with the cream cheese mixture. Keep cold until you serve. Dip the crispy butterscotch cookies in the cranberry dip.

Tip!
You can replace the raisins
with dried blueberries,
strawberries, or other dried
berries and fruits. If you
still haven't had enough of
saffron, you can mix ½ g
(1 packet) with the cream
cheese and cranberries.

CHERRY AND COCONUT FLORENTINES

Crispy and chewy cookies that melt in your mouth like candy. Great with a cup of coffee after dinner or as a beautiful cellophane-wrapped gift.

. . . .

300 g / 10 oz dried cherries
2 ½ dl / 1 ¼ cups light brown sugar
1/3 dl / 5 tsp honey
1 tbsp glucose / corn syrup
200 g / 1 ⅓ sticks butter
2 ½ dl / 1 ¼ cups grated coconut
150 g / 5 oz almond flakes
1 dl / ½ cup white all-purpose flour
250 g / 9 oz chocolate, dark or white

Set the oven to 200 C / 390 F degrees. Cut the cherries into smaller pieces. Melt sugar, honey, corn syrup, and butter on low heat in a thick-bottomed saucepan. Then add coconut, almond flakes, cherries, and flour. Stir into a batter. Line a baking pan that is about 30x40 cm / 12x16 in with parchment paper. Spread the batter evenly in the baking pan. Bake for 12 to 15 minutes or until the cake is golden and crispy. Let it cool completely. Melt the chocolate.

Overturn the cake on parchment paper and remove the paper that is now covering its upside. Spread the melted chocolate on the cake and let it stiffen. Make round cookies by using a cookie cutter, or just carve squares with a knife. It can be hard to push through the cake. A heavy pan or plate on top may help when you are pressing the shapes out.

Tip!

Bake the pastries on two baking sheets. This way you don't have to worry about burning their undersides. If you want you may melt 100g dark chocolate and brush the rings with it. Stack the rings and use the chocolate as "glue." Whether you choose to use chocolate or not, you'll use the frosting to finish decorating the tower.

DANISH NEW YEAR'S TOWER/ KRANSEKAKE

While the bells at the clock tower in Copenhagen bring about the New Year, most Danish people celebrate with champagne and "kransekake." Maybe this Danish tradition is something for you?

12–24 PIECES

500 g / 1 lb marzipan
1 dl / ½ cup powdered sugar
1 egg white

Icing:
2–3 dl / 1–1 ½ cups powdered sugar
1 egg white
A few drops of lemon juice

Set the oven to 225 C / 440 F degrees. Roughly shred the marzipan. Mix marzipan, sugar, and egg white. The dough should be smooth and even. Roll out two long logs, each about 60 cm / 24 in. long. You can either do the traditional wreath cake or a tower. It is easier to roll out the logs if you sprinkle a little powdered sugar on the table. Cut one log in to 15-, 18-, and 27-cm-long pieces, or 6-, 7-, and 10.5-in.-long pieces. Cut other log into pieces that are 12, 21, and 24 cm / 5, 8, and 9.5 in. long. The little piece left over can be used as a small tip on the top of the tower. Form a circle from each piece and place them on two lined baking sheets. Bake the rings for 15 minutes. Let them cool completely before you move them.

Mix powdered sugar and egg whites. Pour the icing in an icing bag that has a small hole. Place the largest ring on a napkin on a plate. Decorate it with zigzag pattern of the icing and stack the rest of the rings on top of each other, decorating each one with the glaze.

RUGELACH

The first time I tried these tasty small pastries was at a Christmas fair when I was ten years old. It took me thirty years to run into them again, and that was in New York. Since then I have baked these for every celebration and holiday in my home. The pastries stem from the Jewish kitchen, where they eat them year round. Serve with spiced apple cider.

30–40 PASTRIES

150 g / 1 ¼ sticks butter (room temperature)

150 g / 5 oz cream cheese (for instance, Philadelphia cream cheese)

1 tbsp powdered sugar

1 pinch of salt

4 dl / 2 cups white all-purpose flour

4 dl / 2 cups apricot jam

150 g / 5 oz walnuts

1 dl / ½ cup granulated sugar

2 tsp cinnamon

200 g / 7 oz raisins

1 egg

> **Tip!**
> You can vary the filling in these pastries freely. Chopped dark or white chocolate, grated almond paste, poppy seeds, and grape jelly are all common.

Mix butter and cream cheese. Blend cinnamon, sugar, salt, and flour. Pour the dry blend into the cream cheese mixture and stir into a batter. Split it into two pieces. Shape the pieces into logs of about 4–5 cm / 2 in. in length. Wrap them in plastic wrap and leave them in the fridge for two hours. Set the oven to 200 C / 390 F degrees. Roll the dough into two rectangles. Spread the jam on top of the two dough pieces. Roast the walnuts in a frying pan on low heat. Let them cool and then crush them lightly and sprinkle them over the jam. Lastly, add the raisins. Roll the dough up, starting from the longest side, and let the two rolls sit in the refrigerator for about 30 minutes. Line two baking sheets with parchment paper. Cut the rolls into slices of about 2 cm / 1 in. Place them on the sheets. Brush them with beaten egg and bake for 25 minutes. After the pastries have cooled sprinkle on powdered sugar and serve.

WINTERY WARM APPLE CIDER

4 GLASSES

1 liter / 5 cups freshly squeezed
    apple juice
4 cloves
10 peppercorns

2 star anise
1 cinnamon stick
½ dl / ¼ cup freshly squeezed
    lemon juice
1–2 tbsp honey

Mix apple juice and spices in a saucepan. Let it come to a boil. Cover
with the lid and let it steep for about 30 minutes with no heat. Strain and
remove the spices. Add the lemon juice, sweeten with honey, and reheat
the drink. Serve.

PHYLLO ROLLS WITH HAZELNUTS

The outside is as crispy as spring rolls, while the center is soft and chewy. These pastries clearly have Middle Eastern influences and go great with a cup of tea.

ABOUT 20 PASTRIES

1 packet phyllo dough, about 250 g / 9 oz

Filling:
200 g / 7 oz hazelnuts
1 dl / ½ cup sugar

2–3 tbsp apricot marmalade
2 tsp ground cinnamon
1 whipped egg white
1 dl / ½ cup melted butter
1 dl / ½ cup thick honey
1 dl / ½ cup sesame seeds

Thaw the phyllo if frozen. Roast the nuts in a dry frying pan. Place them in a clean kitchen towel and rub them against each other so that they let go of their shell. Let the nuts cool completely. Place the nuts and sugar in a food processor and mix until the nuts are evenly distributed. Add apricot marmalade and cinnamon. Set the oven to 175 C / 350 F degrees. Cover the dough with a lightly moist kitchen towel to avoid it drying out. Work with one sheet at a time. Slice the dough into strips of about 10x30 cm / 5x15 in..

Place 1 tbsp of filling on one of the short sides of the strip. Roll a couple of times, then fold the edges inwards and continue to roll the whole strip into a small cigar. Fasten the roll with whipped egg white. Place the roll with the closure downwards on a baking sheet lined with parchment paper. Brush pastries with melted butter and bake for about 20 minutes, or until they have turned golden brown.

Warm the honey so that it's completely fluid. Dip the warm rolls in the honey and sprinkle the sesame seeds on top. Let them dry on a wire rack.

Winterpies, Cheesecakes, and Tarts

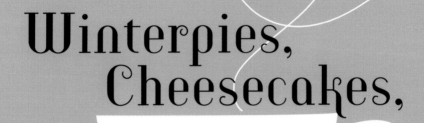

SAFFRON CHEESECAKE ON GINGERBREAD CRUST

This cheesecake will be a great success at your next party, especially because the lovely scent of gingerbread and saffron will spread throughout your home and kitchen while the cake bakes. If you don't want saffron threads in the cake, but prefer an even yellow color, you may let the batter sit for a while in the bowl while you stir now and then. Alternatively, you may warm saffron and ½ dl / ¼ cup sour cream on low heat, then add this to the batter as the recipe explains. Feel free to blend 300 g / 10 oz raspberries and a few tablespoons of powdered sugar and serve with the cake.

8–10 SLICES

75 g / 5 tbsp butter
200 g / 7 oz ginger thins

Filling:
4 eggs
1 dl / ½ cup sugar
2 tbsp white all-purpose flour
600 g / 1.3 lbs cream cheese (for instance,
    Philadelphia cream cheese)
½ g (1 packet) / ⅓–½ tsp saffron
Juice and grated zest of 1 lemon
3 dl / 1 ½ cups sour cream
1 tbsp sugar
1 tsp vanilla sugar

Tip!

In specialty stores that sell spices, chocolate, or baking necessities, you may sometimes be able to find eatable gold leaves. A festive decoration, especially if you are serving the cake for New Year's Eve.

Melt the butter. Crush the ginger thins and mix them in a food processor. Add the butter and mix into an even mass. Fasten a sheet of parchment paper at the bottom of a springform pan of about 24–26 cm / 9–10 in. diameter. Put the mixture into the springform. Set the oven to 175 C / 350 F degrees. Let the springform sit in the fridge while you prepare the filling.

Whisk sugar and eggs until fluffy. Stir in the flour, then add cream cheese, saffron, lemon zest, and juice. Whisk until you have an even batter. Pour the batter into the springform and let it bake for about 45 minutes or until the batter has stiffened. The time will vary depending on the size of your springform.

Stir sour cream, sugar, and vanilla sugar together. Remove the cake from the oven and spread the topping evenly over the cake. Bake for another 5 minutes. Let the cake cool completely before you serve.

NEW YORK CHEESECAKE:
THE QUEEN OF ALL CHEESECAKES

Here's the recipe for a lovely American cheesecake. It contains a lot of cream cheese, but then again it is also enough to serve all of your relatives. The pecan nuts give a different and crispy bottom, and the raspberry jelly is a great contrast, with its sour taste.

14–16 SERVINGS

Crust:
200 g / 7 oz pecan nuts
12 graham crackers
75 g / 5 tbsp butter plus butter for
   greasing the baking pan

Raspberry jelly:
2 gelatin sheets / 3.5 g or ¼ packet
   of powdered gelatin
200 g / 7 oz raspberries
2 tbsp sugar
1–2 pomegranates

Filling:
1 kg / 2.2 lbs cream cheese (for
      instance,
      Philadelphia cream cheese)
4 egg yolks
1 egg
4 dl / 2 cups sugar
2 vanilla beans or 1 tbsp
      vanilla sugar
2 dl / 1 cup sour cream
½ dl / ¼ cup white all-purpose flour

Set the oven to 150 C / 300 F degrees. Generously butter a springform pan of about 24 cm / 9 in. diameter. Then pour the chopped pecans into the form and shake so that the nuts stick to the butter. Crush the cookies by hand or by using a food processor and add the nuts that wouldn't stick to the springform. Melt the butter and stir in the cookies and nuts. Spread the mixture evenly on the bottom of the springform, flatten, and place in the fridge.

Mix cream cheese, egg yolks, the egg, and sugar into a creamy batter. Add the seeds from the vanilla beans or the vanilla sugar and then the sour cream. Sift the flour and add to the batter as well. Pour the batter into the springform. Let it bake for about 1 ½ hours. Let it cool. Place the sheets of gelatin in cold water. Pour the raspberries and sugar into a saucepan.

Warm until the sugar has melted and the juice and meat of the berries are released from the raspberry stems. Drain the raspberries and let the juice pour down into a saucepan. Squeeze the gelatin sheets dry and add them to the juice. Let the sauce cool for a while. Pour the sauce over the cake while it is still in the springform. Let it sit in the fridge for about an hour. Release the cake from the form by scraping around the edges with a knife. Top it with pomegranate seeds. Store in the refrigerator.

Tip!
Instead of pecans you may
use walnuts or other nuts.

CARAMEL CHEESECAKE

Even if the cheesecake might not be the typical holiday pie, it is still great during the winter months. You may decorate this caramel cheese-cake with figs or other winter fruits.

8–10 SERVINGS

Pie crust:

2 dl / 1 cup white all-purpose flour

A pinch of salt

150 g / 1 ¼ sticks butter (room temperature)

½ dl / ¼ cup sugar

1 egg yolk

½ tsp vanilla sugar

100 g / 3.5 oz pecans

Filling:

400 g / 14 oz cream cheese (for instance, Philadelphia cream cheese)

3 large eggs

2 tsp vanilla sugar

3 dl / 1 ½ cups sugar

Chocolate glaze:

100 g / 3.5 oz dark chocolate

½ dl / ¼ cup heavy whipping cream

Set the oven to 175 C / 350 F degrees. Mix flour and salt in a bowl. Whip butter and sugar until light and fluffy. Add the egg yolk and vanilla sugar. Stir in the flour and blend into a dough. Press the dough out in a buttered and floured springform pan with a diameter of about 24 cm / 9 in. Chop the pecan nuts and add them to the bottom as well. Bake the crust for about 20 minutes or until it is golden.

Whip the cream cheese with an electric beater until it has a fluffy texture. Add eggs and vanilla sugar. Pour the sugar into a wide saucepan with a thick bottom. Let the sugar melt while stirring on low heat. Carefully stir the sugar syrup in with the cream cheese. Avoid having the hot sugar mass touch the walls of the bowl. Pour the batter into the springform and let it bake for 45 to 60 minutes. The core of the cake should still be a bit watery when you remove it from the oven. Let it cool for about 30 minutes.

Chop the chocolate. Pour the heavy cream into a saucepan and bring it to a boil. Place the chocolate in a bowl and pour the warm cream on top. Stir until the chocolate is completely melted. Let it sit for a couple of minutes, then stir the chocolate cream until smooth and pour it over the cake. Let it cool completely before you serve.

BANANA CHEESECAKE WITH
CHOCOLATE CRUST

This favorite has a mild and amazingly tasty banana flavor that contrasts nicely with the somewhat sour and fresh-tasting Jell-O topping.

8–10 SLICES
. . . .

Crust:

300 g / 10 oz (2 packets) Oreo cookies

150 g / 1 ¼ sticks butter

Filling:

600 g / 1.3 lbs cream cheese

1 dl / ½ cup sugar

2 ripe bananas

4 eggs

1 tbsp vanilla sugar

Juice of 1 lemon

Topping:

1 dl / ½ cup concentrated tropical juice

2 dl / 1 cup water

5 gelatin sheets (or 8.75 g / 1 packet powdered gelatin)

3 passion fruits

Set the oven to 150 C / 300 F degrees. Split open the Oreos and scrape off the vanilla cream, which you will not be using. Melt the butter. Mix the cookies in a food processor until they are completely crushed. Then add the butter and mix well. Press the mixture out onto a pie pan with detachable sides, diameter 24 cm / 9 in.. Place all of the ingredients for the filling in a food processor and mix into a smooth cream. Pour the cream into the pie pan. Let the pie bake for about 45 minutes or until the cream has stiffened. Let it cool.

Warm the juice and water. Soak the gelatin sheets in cold water for about 5 minutes, then remove the sheets, squeeze them, and let the water drain. Add one at a time to the warm, but not hot, juice. Let the liquid cool and wait until it has started to slightly stiffen. Spread the juice on top of the cake. Place the cake in the fridge and let the topping stiffen and the cake cool completely.

Cut the passion fruits open and scoop the meat over the cake before you serve.

Tip!

Try other kinds of cookies for the crust. Graham crackers
might be the most common cookie used for cheese cakes,
but you may also try chocolate cookies, ginger thins, or oat
cookies. You could also add vanilla, cocoa, grated lemon
zest, or finely chopped nuts to the crust.

ALMOND TART WITH PUNCH CREAM AND NOUGAT

Serve this festive and crispy tart that, despite its polished look, is surprisingly easy to make. This tart is perfect for larger parties and it will keep in the refrigerator for a couple of days. The tart crust is chewy and nutty, while the punch cream is mild and buttery. The almond nougat provides the perfect crunch.

8–10 SLICES

Tart crust:
200 g / 7 oz sweet almonds
2 dl / 1 cup sugar
4 egg whites

Nougat:
1 dl / ½ cup sugar
2 dl / 1 cup chopped sweet almonds

Punch cream:
2 dl / 1 cup heavy whipping cream
4 egg yolks
1 dl / ½ cup sugar
50 g / 3 ½ tbsp butter
1 pinch of salt
3 tbsp fruit punch

Set the oven to 175 C / 350 F degrees. Butter a springform pan with a diameter of about 24–26 cm / 9–10 in.. Line the springform bottom with parchment paper. The reason we butter the form before we line it is to avoid shifting the parchment paper when you add the batter. Also, it becomes easier to loosen the cake from the form once it's done.

Finely grind the almonds or mix them in the food processor for a significant amount of time; this is important in order to make sure that the almonds are properly ground. Mix the ground almonds with the sugar. Beat the egg whites until they start foaming and add the sugar and almond mixture. Scoop the batter into the springform and let it bake for about 30 minutes.

Let the crust cool for a while before removing the paper and placing the crust on a plate. Let it cool completely.

Mix heavy cream, egg yolks, sugar, butter, and fruit punch in a saucepan. Let it simmer while constantly stirring until it becomes a thick cream, making sure it does not boil. Finally, add the pinch of salt and pour the cream into a bowl. The cream might seem a bit thin, but it will thicken after about an hour in the fridge.

While the cream is thickening it is time to prepare the almond nougat. Butter a piece of parchment paper. Pour the sugar into a frying pan. Let it melt on low heat while stirring. Add the almonds when the sugar is light brown and completely melted. Pour the nougat on the parchment paper and let it cool. Break into pieces and roughly chop. Spread the cream evenly on top of the crust and top it off with the nougat.

Keep the tart cool until you serve.

WALNUT AND CHOCOLATE PIE

Walnuts, almond paste, and chocolate: Great ingredients that we often have stacked in our cupboards during the holidays and that may be used for many different kinds of pastries. This pie is compact and heavy and is best served in smaller pieces. It tastes wonderful with a warm beverage, and it will keep for a long time.

8–10 Slices

Pie dough:
125 g / 1 stick butter (cold)
1 dl / ½ cup sugar
1 egg
4 dl / 2 cups white all-purpose flour

Walnut filling:
150 g / 5 oz almond paste or marzipan
2 dl / 1 cup sugar

125 g / 1 stick butter
   (room temperature)
2 eggs
2 tbsp white all-purpose flour
100 g / 3.5 oz dark chocolate
200 g / 7 oz walnuts or hazelnuts

Decoration:
About 75 g / 2.5 oz dark chocolate

Place all of the ingredients for the dough in a food processor and mix into a large ball. Flatten and wrap it in plastic wrap. Let it sit in the refrigerator for at least half an hour. Set the oven to 200 C / 390 F degrees. Butter and flour a springform pan with a diameter of about 26 cm / 10 in. Roll the dough out in between two sheets of plastic wrap. Place the dough in the springform and flatten evenly.

Roughly grate the almond paste and stir in the sugar. Add the butter and work it until even. Stir in the eggs one at a time. Blend flour, chopped chocolate, and roughly chopped nuts and add them to the batter. Pour the batter into the piecrust. Let it bake for about 40 minutes or until the filling is stiff; it will feel rubbery when you press down with a finger. Let the cake cool before you melt the chocolate and drizzle it over the cake. You may serve with a spoonful of whipped cream and some cocoa powder.

Tip!
You can keep the pie in the
refrigerator, but let it sit
at room temperature for an
hour before you serve.

WHITE CHOCOLATE PIE WITH FIGS

I first tasted this fantastic chocolate pie in London in a small store named Books for Cooks, which sells cookbooks from all over the world. The combination of sticky white chocolate, sweet liqueur, and figs is wonderful. The pie is at its best if you let it stand for a while at room temperature before you slice it. Do not keep it in the oven for too long. The rule here, as with any such pie, is that it should be removed from the oven right when the batter has "stiffened" but still moves a little when you nudge the baking pan.

12 SLICES

250 g / 9 oz white chocolate

250 g / 2 sticks unsalted butter
   (room temperature)

3 ½ dl / 1 ⅓ cups sugar

4 eggs

1 ⅓ dl / ⅓ cups buttermilk

3 dl / 1 ½ cups white all-purpose flour

2 tsp baking powder

1¼ dl / ¾ cup dry sherry

Chocolate glaze:

1 ¼ dl / ⅔ cup heavy
   whipping cream

Grated zest of 1 lemon

200 g / 7 oz white chocolate

Fresh figs

Set the oven to 175 C / 350 F degrees. Line the bottom and sides of a buttered springform, about 24 cm / 9 in. in diameter, with parchment paper. The springform needs to be buttered so that the paper stays in place.

Melt the chocolate on low heat in a saucepan or in the microwave. You need to be careful with white chocolate as it burns easily. Whip butter and sugar together into a white and fluffy batter. Add the beaten eggs slowly. Whisk well. Add the butter milk to the mixture. Scoop in the flour mixed with baking powder while stirring. Add half of the sherry and the cool, melted chocolate. Pour the batter into the springform and bake for 1 to 1 ½ hours. The pie is finished when no liquid batter sticks to a toothpick.

However, some small crumbles should still stick, as it should be a little chewy in the middle. You may have to cover the pie with some aluminum foil after 45 minutes, when it starts gaining some color.

Remove the pie and let it rest in the pan for about 25 minutes. Overturn the pie onto a wire rack and place a plate underneath that will catch any left over liqueur. Pour the remaining liqueur evenly over the warm pie.

Boil the heavy cream and lemon zest. Remove the saucepan from the oven and let it sit for about 30 minutes. Strain the lemon zest. Break the chocolate into pieces. Bring the cream to a boil once more and pour it over the chocolate. Let it stand for about 5 minutes until the chocolate is completely melted. Stir slowly and let it cool. Pour the chocolate cream over the pie when it is completely cool and place it in a cool place so that the glaze may stiffen. Serve with fresh figs. You may sprinkle some powdered sugar on top before serving.

TORTA DELLA NONNA

"Torta Della Nonna" means "grandmother's cake" in Italian, and almost every Italian family has their own recipe. Feel free to mix this dough by hand, as the heat from your hands is great for the dough.

8–10 SLICES
. . . .

Filling:
1 vanilla bean
2 ½ dl / 1 ¼ cups milk
5 egg yolks
1 dl / ½ cup sugar
½ dl / ¼ cup ricotta cheese
2 tbsp white all-purpose flour
optional: 2 tbsp Cointreau (citrus liqueur)

Dough:
4 dl / 2 cups white all-purpose
    flour
1 ¼ dl / ⅔ cup sugar
1 tsp baking powder
¼ tsp salt
8 tbsp diced cold butter
1 egg
1 tsp vanilla extract

For brushing:
1 egg plus some water
25 g / 0.8 oz pine nuts
powdered sugar

Slice the vanilla bean in two down the middle. Scrape out the seeds. Put the seeds and the bean in the milk. Heat the milk in a saucepan with a thick bottom. Bring it to a boil and then remove from the stove right away.

Whisk egg yolks, sugar, and ricotta cheese into a white and fluffy batter in a bowl. Add the flour a little at a time. Remove the vanilla bean from the milk and throw it out. Stir the milk into the batter. Pour the batter back into the saucepan. Heat it while stirring and bring it to a boil, then let it simmer for a minute while stirring. Then put the cream into a bowl and add the Cointreau if desired. Cover the bowl with plastic wrap and let it sit in the refrigerator for an hour.

Set the oven to 175 C / 350 F degrees. Butter a springform with a diameter of about 24 cm / 9 in. Mix white all-purpose flour, sugar, baking powder, and salt and then work in the butter. Blend by hand or with a mixer. Lastly, stir in the beaten egg and vanilla sugar. Split the dough in half. Cover the springform with one of the halves. Press the dough about 2 ½ cm / 1 in. up the walls of the form. Pour the cream into the form. The dough should rise about 1 cm / ½ in. above the cream filling.

Roll out the other half of the dough on a table covered with flour. If it is hard to work with you may use two sheets of plastic wrap to help roll it out. Cover the cream with the dough lid and pinch the edges together. It may look a little lumpy and ugly, but this will even out once it bakes.

Beat the egg with some water and brush the dough lid with the mixture. Sprinkle pine nuts on top. Create small slits in the lid with a sharp knife so that the steam may escape during baking. Bake for 35 minutes or until the cake is golden brown. Let it cool and cover it with a generous amount of powdered sugar.

Tip!

If you wish, you may flavor the cream with chocolate instead of liqueur. Melt 50 g / 1.7 oz dark chocolate on low heat. Stir the melted chocolate in with the vanilla cream. If you want an even stronger chocolate taste you may add 2–3 tbsp of cocoa powder in the flour when you do the cake dough.

APFEL STRUDEL WITH GINGERBREAD ICECREAM

Apple is always a tasty ingredient in pastries and may be used year-round. If possible, use Swedish, sour, winter apples. The apfel strudel makes me think of ski slopes and Austria. This is a simplified version. Serve with gingerbread ice-cream.

4–6 SERVINGS

Gingerbread ice cream:
5 dl / 2 ½ cups milk
1 tbsp gingerbread spices
½ dl / ¼ cup dark brown sugar
1 pinch of salt
1 dl / ½ cup sugar
2 eggs

Apfel strudel:
4–5 sheets phyllo dough

1 dl / ½ cup breadcrumbs
1 dl / ½ cup finely chopped almonds
1 tbsp plus ½ dl / ¼ cup butter
4 sour apples
½ dl / ¼ cup raw cane sugar
1–2 tsp cinnamon
½ dl / ¼ cup raisins
Finely grated lemon zest of 1 lemon
½ dl / ¼ cup roughly chopped almonds
2 tbsp powdered sugar

Pour milk, spices, brown sugar, salt, and ½ dl / ¼ cup of the sugar in a saucepan. Let it come to a boil and continue to let it simmer for about 10 minutes. Remove the saucepan from the heat and let it cool. Whisk eggs and the rest of the sugar until white and fluffy. Stir in the milk mixture. Warm the batter and whip until it thickens. The temperature should be about 82 C / 180 F degrees. Remove it from the stove and stir the batter.

Let the batter sit in the fridge until it is completely cool. Stir now and then. Freeze the ice cream batter in an ice cream maker until it obtains the right creamy texture. Scoop it into a cool bowl. Let it sit in the freezer for another couple of hours.

Thaw the phyllo dough if it is frozen. Fry breadcrumbs and almonds in 1 tablespoon of butter until the almonds are lightly browned. Set aside.

Peel, pit, and dice the apples. Mix apples, sugar, cinnamon, raisins, lemon zest, and the roughly chopped almonds in a bowl. Set the oven to 200 C / 390 F degrees. Melt the rest of the butter. Roll out the phyllo dough on the kitchen counter.

First, brush one sheet with melted butter. Then layer another sheet on top and brush again. Repeat until you have layered all of the sheets. Blend the browned breadcrumbs and almonds with the apple mixture. Spread it evenly on top of the phyllo dough. Roll the sheets up into a compact log and place it in a buttered baking pan. Bake for 20 to 25 minutes or until the strudel is crispy and golden. Sift some powdered sugar on top and serve with the ice cream.

CHOCOLATE-TRUFFLE PIE
WITH PEAR AND GINGER MARMALADE

The pie crust is crispy with an intense chocolate flavor. Between the crust and the creamy chocolate truffle is the strong, sweet, and spicy pear marmalade. This exciting flavor combination of sweet chocolate, fresh pears, and spicy ginger is unique.

Feel free to make the marmalade a couple of days in advance. Peel and pit the pears. Dice them. Roughly chop the pickled ginger. Mix all the ingredients together and let it come to a boil. Let the marmalade simmer for about 20 minutes. Pour in clean jars with lids and keep in the fridge.

10–12 pieces

Pear and ginger marmalade:
2 kg / 4.5 lbs ripe pears
100 g / 3.5 oz pickled ginger
Zest and juice of 1 lemon
1–2 tsp finely grated fresh ginger
1 kg / 2.2 lbs sugar

Pie crust:
3 dl / 1 ½ cups white all-purpose flour
½ dl / ¼ cup sugar
100 g / 7 tbsp unsalted butter
1 egg yolk
3 tbsp cocoa

Chocolate-truffle filling:
250 g / 2 sticks unsalted
  butter
250 g / 9 oz dark chocolate
3 dl / 1 ½ cups sugar
4 egg yolks
3 tbsp cocoa
1 dl / ½ cup white all-purpose
  flour
A pinch of salt
4 egg whites

Mix the ingredients for the crust together in a food processor or by hand. If needed, add 1–2 tbsp of water. Knead the dough together and let it rest for 30 minutes in the fridge. Set the oven to 225 C / 440 F degrees. Roll out the dough and place it in a buttered pie dish of about 26 cm / 10 in. diameter. Prick the bottom with a fork. Pinch the edges together with the help of aluminum foil so that the dough doesn't fall down. Let it bake for 10 to 15 minutes. Remove the pie crust from the oven and lower the temperature to 150 C / 300 F degrees.

Melt the butter and chocolate on very low heat in a saucepan. Stir in the sugar and let it cool somewhat. Add the yolks one at a time. Whisk the egg whites and add to the batter.

Spread about 1 dl / ½ cup of marmalade over the pie crust and pour the batter on top. Bake the pie for about 50 minutes.

CARAMEL PIE WITH CHOCOLATE TRUFFLE

A praline pie with a heavenly dark chocolate truffle topping. Serve the pie in small pieces as confectionery or in pie slices with coffee after dinner

8–10 slices
....

Crust:
5 dl / 1 ½ cups white all-purpose flour
100 g / 7 tbsp butter
2 tbsp sugar
1 yolk

Caramel filling:
1 vanilla bean
2 dl / 1 cup heavy whipping cream
1 ½ dl / ⅓ cup sugar
1 dl / ½ cup light corn syrup
2 tbsp brown sugar
2 tbsp honey
200 g / 1 ⅓ sticks butter

Chocolate truffle:
200 g / 7 oz dark chocolate
1 dl / ½ cup heavy whipping cream
2 tbsp butter

Set the oven to 200 C / 390 F degrees. Mix all the ingredients for the crust in a food processor and let it run until the dough forms a lump. Roll out the dough and press it onto a pie dish with a removable bottom of about 26 cm / 10 in. diameter. Prebake the crust for about 20 minutes. Cut the vanilla bean down the middle and scrape out the seeds. Mix the vanilla bean, seeds, whipping cream, sugar, corn syrup, brown sugar, and honey in a sauce pan. Let it simmer on low heat for about 25 minutes. Remove the vanilla bean and throw it out. Add the butter in increments while you stir it into what is now the caramel filling. Let the filling cool for a while.

Pour the cream into the pie dish and place the pie in the fridge. Break the chocolate into pieces and melt it over a double boiler or in the microwave. Bring whipping cream and butter to a boil. Pour the mixture into the melted chocolate while stirring. Let the chocolate truffle cream cool for a while. Spread a layer of truffle on top of the caramel filling. Store the pie in the fridge.

Cakes
and
Muffins

RED VELVET CAKE

The American Red Velvet Cake originally sprung from New Orleans. Throughout the years it has been called a multitude of names, including Devil's Food Cake, Waldorf Astoria Cake, and 100 Dollar Cake. Although we now obtain the characteristic red color by the use of food coloring, it is assumed that the color was originally a result of the cocoa, which used to be processed differently and thus had a more reddish color. Another theory is that the cake used to contain beetroots.

12–16 PIECES
· · · · · · · · · · ·

Cake:

1 ⅓ cups sugar

1 ⅓ sticks of butter

3 eggs

2 cups of white all-purpose flour

1 tsp baking powder

½ tsp salt

¼ cup cocoa

2 tsp vanilla sugar

1 ¼ cups buttermilk

1-2 tbsp red food coloring

1 tsp vinegar

Cream cheese frosting:

8 oz cream cheese

8 oz mascarpone cheese

1 tsp vanilla sugar

Powdered sugar

2 cups heavy whipping cream

Set the oven to 175 C / 350 F degrees. Butter a 9 in. round cake pan. Use an electric beater to whisk the egg and sugar for about 5 minutes so that you get a creamy batter. Add the eggs one by one and mix together. Blend all the dry ingredients in a separate bowl. Sift the dry ingredients into the batter. Blend the buttermilk, food coloring, and vinegar in a bowl and add to the batter; stir it evenly. Pour the batter into the cake pan and bake for about 40 minutes or until a testing toothpick is dry. Let it cool for a little while and then turn it out on a baking grid. Let it cool completely. Place all the ingredients for the frosting, except the whipping cream, in a food processor. Mix well. Whisk the cream and add it to the cream cheese mixture in batches. If the frosting is not stiff enough you may place it in the refrigerator until it gains the necessary texture. You may let the cake sit in the fridge overnight before serving.

CHOCOLATE CAKE WITH
COFFEE SYRUP AND DATES

*I highly recommend this fantastic cake for the true lover of chocolate.
The texture is compact, but still airy, not as chewy or sticky as brownies.
The coffee syrup and dates add an additional dimension of taste.*

Cake:
225 g / 2 sticks butter
200 g / 7 oz dark chocolate (70 percent)
2 dl / 1 cup cocoa
2 large eggs
3 dl / 1 ½ cups sugar
2 dl / 1 cup raw cane sugar
2 tsp vanilla sugar

1 pinch of salt
200 g / 7 oz extra fine white all-purpose flour
2 ½ dl / 1 ¼ cup boiling water
1–2 pitted dates cut in halves

Coffee syrup:
½ dl / ¼ cup strong coffee (for instance, espresso)
2 dl / 1 cup sugar
1 whole star anise
2 tbsp Kahlua or another coffee liqueur

Set the oven to 175 C / 350 F degrees. Butter and flour a baking pan of about 2 liters or a pan that is 8x8x3 in., or slightly more than 2 quarts. Break the chocolate into pieces. Melt butter and chocolate on low heat in a saucepan with a thick bottom. Stir in the cocoa. Whip eggs, sugars, vanilla sugar, and salt together. It shouldn't become white and fluffy; just make sure it is blended well.

Stir the mixture in with the melted chocolate. Add the flour a little at a time. Pour the hot water into the batter while you are whisking. Scoop it into the baking pan and bake for about 45 minutes.

Pour coffee, sugar, and the whole star anise into a saucepan with a thick bottom. Heat it up so that the sugar melts. Do not stir around too much. When the sugar has melted, raise the heat and let the mixture boil for 2 to 3 minutes until it has thickened. Add the liqueur. Remove the pot from the stove.

Make small holes in the cake with the help of a small toothpick. Pour half of the coffee syrup over the cake, especially the holes. Serve the cake lukewarm with dates, the rest of the lukewarm coffee syrup, and whipped cream.

GINGERBREAD SQUARES WITH CREAM CHEESE AND LINGONBERRY

Exotic spices, like cinnamon, cardamom, ginger, and clove, help create one of the most Swedish cakes there is: the soft gingerbread cake. The sharp cream cheese topping gives the cake a fresh taste.

ABOUT 16 SQUARES

Gingerbread cake:

200 g / 1 ⅓ sticks butter (room temperature)

4 dl / 2 cups sugar

4 eggs

3 dl / 1 ½ cups sour cream

4 dl / 2 cups white all-purpose flour

2–3 tbsp gingerbread spices

2 tbsp baking soda

Frosting:

200 g / 7 oz cream cheese (for instance, Philadelphia cream cheese)

50 g / 3 ½ tbsp butter (room temperature)

2 dl / 1 cup powdered sugar

2 tsp vanilla sugar

2–3 dl / 1–1 ½ cup frozen lingonberries for garnish

Set the oven to 175 C / 350 F degrees. Whisk butter and sugar until fluffy. Stir in one egg at a time. Add the sour cream. Blend flour, spices, and baking soda. Stir it all together into an even batter. Line a baking pan with high sidewalls, about 30x40 cm / 12x16 in. Pour the batter in the pan. Let it bake for about 30 minutes. Mix all the ingredients for the frosting. Let the cake cool completely and cover it with the frosting. Cut the cake into squares and top it off with the lingonberries.

BANANA AND HAZELNUT CAKE

*This banana cake is really tasty. It's juicy and crunchy thanks to the ha-
zelnuts. If you want a stronger chocolate taste you can add 100 g / 3.5 oz
chopped chocolate of any kind.*

8–10 PIECES

Cake:

2 large or 3 small bananas

2 dl / 1 cup sugar

1 dl / ½ cup hazelnuts

100 g / 7 tbsp butter

1 egg

2 tbsp heavy cream

2 ½ dl / 1 ¼ cups white all-purpose flour

1 tbsp vanilla sugar

1 tsp baking powder

1 tsp baking soda

Chocolate glaze:

100 g / 3.5 oz milk, dark, or
   white chocolate

Caramelized nuts:

100 g / 3.5 oz hazelnuts

2–3 tbsp sugar

Begin with the caramelized nuts: Place a buttered piece of parchment
paper on the kitchen counter. Roast the hazelnuts in a dry frying pan until
they start giving off a nutty scent and their shell is loosening. Rub the nuts
in a clean kitchen towel. Melt sugar in the frying pan. When the sugar has
turned brown add the nuts to the pan. Place onto the parchment paper.
Separate the nuts with a fork and let them cool.

Set the oven to 200 C / 390 F degrees. Whisk mashed bananas and
sugar together. Grind the nuts in a nut grinder. Melt the butter. Stir the
banana mixture, egg, cream, butter, and ground nuts together. Mix the dry
ingredients together and add them to the banana batter. Butter a baking
pan and sprinkle with breadcrumbs; the pan should be no smaller than 24
cm / 9 in. in diameter. Pour the batter into the pan and let it bake for about
30 minutes. Remove the cake and let it cool. Melt the chocolate on low
heat in a saucepan. Scoop the chocolate over the cake. Sprinkle the nuts
on top before the chocolate cools completely.

CHERRY AND ALMOND CAKE WITH CHOCOLATE TOPPING

This cake is like a chocolate praline with a grown-up flavor: almond, chocolate, rum, and cherries. A luxurious cake with a long shelf life.

10–12 SLICES

2 ½ dl / 1 ¼ cups sugar
200 g / 1 ⅓ sticks butter
4 eggs
200 g / 7 oz almonds
100 g / 3.5 oz dark chocolate
½ dl / ¼ cup light or dark rum
2 tsp baking powder
1 ½ dl / ⅓ cup white all-purpose flour

300 g / 10 oz fresh cherries, or 250 g / 9 oz jarred cherries, or 250 g / 9 oz cherry jam with whole berries

Chocolate topping:
1 dl / ½ cup milk
200 g / 7 oz dark chocolate
2 egg yolks
50 g / 3 ½ tbsp butter (room temperature)

Set the oven to 175 C / 350 F degrees. Butter a springform, 24–26 cm / 9–10 in. diameter. Line it with parchment paper. Whisk sugar and butter until white and fluffy. Stir in the eggs one at a time. Grind the almonds in a nut grinder or in a food processor. Roughly chop the chocolate. Add ground almonds, chocolate chunks, and rum into the butter mixture. Stir until it is blended well. Mix flour and baking powder and add it to the batter as well.

Pit the cherries if you are using fresh berries. Lastly, add the berries to the batter. Scoop the batter into the springform and bake for about 45 minutes or until nothing sticks to the testing toothpick.

Loosen the cake from the form and let it cool on a grid. Warm the milk in a saucepan. Break the chocolate into pieces and let it melt in the milk. Beat the yolks in a bowl. Stir half of the chocolate blend into the bowl. Then pour the mixture back into the saucepan with the remaining chocolate blend. Let it simmer for 1 to 2 minutes while you stir vigorously. Finally, add the butter in pieces. Let the cake and chocolate frosting cool completely before you cover the cake with the frosting. Keep the cake cool before serving.

Tip!

Maybe you are now excited to finally take advantage of your freezer full of pitted cherries? If not, you can save the following recipe for summertime: Mix 500 g pitted cherries, 200 g / 7 oz, sugar and 50 g / 3 ½ tbsp butter in a saucepan. Let it come to a boil and serve the sauce warm or cold. The sauce tastes amazing with Greek yogurt, ice cream, or rice porridge for Christmas.

CARROT MUFFINS WITH LIME CRÈME

To change things up a bit it might be nice to serve the beloved carrot cake as muffins. They are almost like mini pastries. The carrots and nuts make the muffins especially juicy and they keep for a very long time. When I bake muffins I use muffin cups in muffin pans that you may get in many different sizes. The volume may vary from ½ to 2 dl / 1 cup batter. Bake large muffins in 150–175 C / 300–350 F degrees for 20 to 40 minutes. Bake smaller muffins in 200–225 C / 390–440 F degrees for 12 to 20 minutes. They easily become dry if they bake for too long.

ABOUT 14 SMALLER MUFFINS

3 dl / 1 ½ cups extra fine white
   all-purpose flour
1 tbsp ground cinnamon
2 dl / 1 cup sugar
3 eggs
175 g / 1 ½ sticks butter
   (room temperature) or
   2 dl / 1 cup canola oil
3 dl / 1 ½ cups grated carrots
50 g / 1.7 oz walnuts

Frosting:
300 g / 10 oz cream cheese (for
   instance, Philadelphia cream
   cheese)
150 g / 1 ¼ sticks butter
   (room temperature)
4 dl / 2 cups powdered sugar
1 tbsp vanilla sugar
Zest and juice of 2–3 limes or 1 lemon

Set the oven to 200 C / 390 F degrees. Mix the dry ingredients in a bowl. Add eggs and butter. Whisk until the batter is even. Pour the carrots and roughly chopped nuts into the batter. Scoop the batter into muffin cups. Bake for 15 to 20 minutes in the middle of the oven. Test whether or not the muffins are ready by pressing on them lightly with a finger. They should feel bouncy and not rubbery.

Stir or whisk all of the ingredients for the frosting together. Add frosting on top of each of the cooled muffins. Decorate with walnut halves or sprinkles.

SNOWY MADELEINE CAKES

Serve a snow-covered hill of snack-sized Madeleine cakes. Marcel Proust made the cake famous in his work "In Search of Lost Time," in which the scent and taste of the madeleine cake dipped in linden blossom reawakened his childhood memories. The cakes are traditionally baked in molded shell shapes, but you may of course use other kinds of metal cookie molds or muffin cups as well. The molds should be brushed with generous amounts of butter to give the cakes the right taste.

250 g / 2 sticks butter

6 eggs

3 dl / 1 ½ cups sugar

Finely grated zest and juice of
 1 lemon

4 ½ dl / 2 cups white all-purpose
 flour

1 dl / ½ cup butter

2–3 tbsp powdered sugar

Set the oven to 200 C / 390 F degrees. Melt the butter in a saucepan and set it to the side. Separate the egg whites and yolks. Beat the yolks with the sugar until white and fluffy. Stir in the melted butter, lemon zest, and juice, then carefully add the flour a little at a time. Whisk the egg whites until fluffy and add them into the batter. Brush the molds with butter and fill the shapes with the batter so that they are half full. Bake in the middle of the oven for about 12 minutes. Let the cakes cool somewhat and sprinkle powdered sugar on top.

COMFORTING CHOCOLATE DRINK

4–6 GLASSES
....

1 1/5 cups milk

1 cinnamon stick

3–4 whole, dried piri-piri chilies

200 g / 7 oz dark chocolate

1 dl / ½ cup fruit or berry liqueur

2 dl / 1 cup heavy whipping cream

cocoa

Pour the milk in a saucepan. Add crushed cinnamon and the whole chilies. Let it come to a boil. Let it simmer for about 5 minutes. Strain the cinnamon and chili. Roughly chop the chocolate and add it to the warm milk. Let the drink come to a boil once more. Remove it from the stove and add the liqueur. Whip the cream. Serve the hot chocolate with a spoonful of whipped cream sprinkled with cocoa powder.

Tip!

You may also make muffins or other small pastries with this batter. Decorate with a spoonful of yogurt crème: Mix 200 g / 7 oz Philadelphia cream cheese, 2 dl / 1 cup drained yogurt or creamy Greek yogurt, ½ dl / ¼ cup powdered sugar, 1 tbsp vanilla sugar, and 1 tbsp lemon juice.

FRESH ORANGE CAKE

When you bake this wintery, beautiful cake, cardamom and the scent of orange spreads throughout the kitchen as a concentrate of holiday scents.

8–10 SLICES

Glazed orange wedges:

3 oranges

100 g / 3.5 oz sugar

Cake:

200 g / 1 ⅓ sticks unsalted butter

4 dl / 2 cups sugar

5 eggs

2 tsp ground cardamom

2 tbsp black poppy seeds

5 dl / 2 ½ cups white all-purpose flour

2 tsp baking powder

½ tsp salt

2 dl / 1 cup butter milk or sour cream

2 tbsp concentrated orange juice

Juice and grated zest of 1 orange

Butter and bread crumbles for the baking pan

Glaze:

100 g / 3.5 oz powdered sugar

1 tbsp orange juice

Peel and split two of the oranges into slices. Melt the sugar in a saucepan with a thick bottom on medium heat. Don't stir, but lightly shake the pot so that the sugar covers the entire bottom of the saucepan. Squeeze the juice of half of the third orange. Carefully pour the juice into the sugar. Let it come to a boil; you should then have a golden caramel. Add the orange slices and remove the saucepan from the stove. Let the slices sit in the caramel for 10 minutes, then take them out and place them on parchment paper. Throw out the remaining caramel.

Set the oven to 175 C / 350 F degrees. Whisk sugar and butter until white and fluffy. Add the eggs one at a time. Mix the dry ingredients in a bowl. Add the dry ingredients to the egg mixture. Lastly, pour in the butter milk, concentrated juice, zest, and juice. Mix well. Butter a baking pan and sprinkle breadcrumbs to cover it. The pan should hold 1 ½–2 L / 7 ½–10 cups. Pour the batter into the pan and bake for about an hour. The cake is ready when nothing sticks to a test toothpick.

Mix a thick glaze out of powdered sugar and juice from the remaining orange half. Cover the warm cake with the white glaze. Decorate with the orange slices. Let the cake cool before you slice it.

CINNAMON BROWNIE WITH SAFFRON FROSTING

In Sweden we call a soft and chewy chocolate cake "kladdkaka," but in the United States this kind of cake is called a brownie. Many American children enjoy brownies during holidays and other celebrations.

ABOUT 12 PIECES

Chocolate batter:
150 g / 5 oz dark chocolate (70 percent)
200 g / 1 ⅓ sticks butter
4 dl / 2 cups sugar
4 eggs
1 tbsp cinnamon
2 dl / 1 cup white all-purpose flour
100 g / 3.5 oz shelled pistachios

Saffron frosting:
¼ g (1 / 2 packet) / ⅛ tsp saffron
1 dl / ½ cup heavy whipping cream
200 g / 7 oz white chocolate

Set the oven to 200 C / 390 F degrees. Butter a baking pan, about 20x30 cm / 8x12 in. Chop the chocolate and melt it with the butter in a saucepan on low heat. Whisk sugar, eggs, and cinnamon together in a bowl so that you get a light and fluffy batter. Pour the melted chocolate into the bowl and mix well. Add sifted flour and stir until the batter is even. Chop the pistachio nuts and add them to the batter as well. Pour the batter into the buttered baking pan and bake for about 25 minutes. The cake should be chewy on the inside but stiff on the outside. Let it cool. Bring heavy cream and saffron to a boil. Remove the saucepan from the stove. Let it stew for about 30 minutes. Let it come to a boil once more and remove it from the stove. Chop the chocolate and stir it in with the saffron cream. Let the frosting cool somewhat before you spread it out on top of the cake.

CHEWY CHOCOLATE MUFFINS WITH FUDGE AND COCONUT

Attractive small muffins with a chewy middle. Serve them lukewarm with cold whipped cream or vanilla ice cream. You may also sprinkle some coconut flakes or grated coconut on top.

12–16 MUFFINS

Muffins:
200 g / 1 ⅓ sticks butter
4 eggs
5 dl / 2 ½ cups sugar
2 ½ dl / 1 ¼ cups white all-purpose flour
1 dl / ½ cup grated coconut
1 tbsp vanilla sugar

1 pinch of salt
1 ½ dl / ⅓ cup cocoa
½–1 dl / ¼–½ cup coconut flakes

Fudge frosting:
100 g / 3.5 oz dark chocolate
25 g / 5 tsp butter
2 tbsp light corn syrup
½ dl / ¼ cup heavy cream

Set the oven to 200 C / 390 F degrees. Melt the butter. Mix the eggs and sugar. Don't whisk it to be too fluffy. Stir the butter in with the eggs and sugar. Blend the dry ingredients and add them to the batter. Stir until even. Fill the muffin cups about ¾ full and bake them for 8 to 10 minutes, no longer. Roughly chop the chocolate. Bring corn syrup, butter, and cream to a boil. Remove the saucepan from the stove and stir in the chocolate. Scoop the chocolate sauce over the muffins when they have cooled for a bit.

BROWNIES WITH COCONUT TOSCA

Chewy chocolate brownie covered in a coconut tosca as crispy as hard caramel. Feel free to prepare an extra batch; they usually disappear from the coffee table at the blink of an eye. You may also freeze them.

16–20 BROWNIES

Cake:

200 g / 1 ⅓ sticks butter

4 eggs

6 dl / 3 cups sugar

1 dl / ½ cup cocoa

2 pinches of salt

1 tbsp vanilla sugar

3 dl / 1 ½ cups white all-purpose flour

Coconut tosca:

200 g / 7 oz coconut flakes

2 dl / 1 cup sugar

1 dl / ½ cup light corn syrup

1 ½ dl / ⅓ cup heavy whipping cream

75 g / 5 tbsp butter

Set the oven to 200 C / 390 F degrees. Butter a baking pan with elevated edges that is about 30x40 cm / 12x16 in. Line it with parchment paper. Melt the butter in a saucepan. Whisk eggs and sugar until white and fluffy with an electric beater. Add cocoa, salt, vanilla sugar, and white all-purpose flour. Stir into an even batter. Add the melted butter and pour the batter into the baking pan. Bake for about 10 minutes. While the cake is baking, blend coconut, sugar, corn syrup, cream, and butter in a saucepan. Let it boil into a thick batter while stirring. Remove the cake from the oven and cover it with the coconut batter. Let the cake bake for an additional 10 to 15 minutes. Let it cool completely before you cut it into squares.

Wheatbread and Buns

SAFFRON BREAD WITH QUARK

No celebration is complete without the holiday's own wheat bread. Not to mention the fact that the unique sweet scent of saffron will always get you in a celebratory mood.

The quark cheese gives the bread a longer shelf-life, and the loaves are moister than smaller buns like "lussekatter" or saffron buns. If you choose to make "lussekatter," set the oven to 225 C / 440 F degrees.

4 LOAVES

1 g (2 packets) / 1 ½ tsp saffron

5 dl / 2 ½ cups milk

100 g / 7 tbsp butter

50 g / 2 tbsp yeast

250 g / 9 oz quark cheese (can substitute fromage frais or cottage cheese)

½ tsp salt

2 dl / 1 cup sugar

1 dl / ½ cup large raisins or currants

2 eggs

14–15 dl / 7–7 ½ cups white all-purpose flour

2–3 tbsp granulated sugar

Stir the saffron in with ½ dl / ¼ cup lukewarm milk. Melt the butter in a saucepan. Pour the rest of the milk and the saffron milk into the saucepan as well. Let it become lukewarm. Crumble the yeast in a bowl and dissolve it in the lukewarm milk. Stir in the quark, salt, sugar, raisins, and one egg. Add most of the flour and work the dough so that the ingredients are mixed well. Let it rise for about 30 minutes.

Put the dough onto a lightly floured table and knead it. Divide the dough into 12 equally sized pieces and roll them into logs about 30 cm / 12 in. long. Attach the logs in threes and braid them together. Pinch the ends together and tuck them in under the braid. Place the braids on lined or buttered baking sheets. Set the oven to 200 C / 390 F degrees. Let the braids rise for another 30 minutes. Beat the other egg and use it to brush the loaves before they go in the oven. Sprinkle sugar on top. Bake in the lower part of the oven for 15 to 20 minutes.

CINNAMON ROLLS

Even though many proclaim that the cinnamon bun is originally from Sweden, this is actually a traditional American recipe. Amazingly fluffy buns with a creamy filling of pecan nuts, cinnamon, and brown sugar. The buns will be crisper if you don't melt the butter but rather work it into the dough as described in the recipe.

ABOUT 40 BUNS

Dough:
25 g / 1 ¼ tbsp yeast
5 dl / 2 ½ cups milk (room temperature)
½ tsp salt
1 ½ dl / ¾ cup sugar
1 egg
About 15 dl / 7 ½ cups white
    all-purpose flour
150 g / 1 ¼ sticks butter
1 egg for brushing

Filling:
3 dl / 1 ½ cups pecan nuts
150 g / 1 ¼ sticks butter (room
    temperature)
1 ½ dl / ⅓ cup brown sugar
2 tbsp ground cinnamon
1 tbsp vanilla sugar

Frosting:
2 ½ dl / 1 ¼ cups powdered sugar
½ tsp vanilla sugar
1–2 tbsp orange juice

Crumble the yeast in a bowl and pour in the milk. Add salt, sugar, and egg and whisk well. Pour the flour in the bowl as well and work into dough. Lastly, add the butter and knead the dough until even. Let the dough rise for about two hours, or until the size of the dough has doubled.

Chop the nuts. Put 1 dl / ½ cup of the nuts aside. Stir all of the ingredients for the filling together by hand or with a food processor. Put the dough on a lightly floured table and knead until it no longer sticks to the table or your hands. If needed, you may add extra flour, but avoid letting the dough become too compact. Divide the dough into two equal parts and roll them out into two rectangular sheets of about 30x40 cm / 12x16 in.

Cover the dough sheets with the filling and roll them together, starting from the longest side. Slice the rolls pieces into 2–3 cm / 1 in. thick. Place the buns in paper cups or on a buttered or lined baking sheet. Set the oven to 250 C / 480 F degrees. Let the buns rise for an additional 30 minutes. Brush them with egg. Decorate with the remaining chopped pecan nuts. Bake in the oven for 8 to10 minutes. Let the buns cool. Stir the frosting together and drizzle it over the buns. (See picture on p. 103.)

VANILLA KRINGLES

Fluffy and vanilla-scented kringles are a type of Nordic pretzel and are a great fit for most occasions year round. You'll get the world's best saffron kringles if you add one packet of saffron to the milk.

ABOUT 30 KRINGLES
· · · · · · · · · · · · · · · · ·

Kringles:
200 g / 1 ⅓ sticks butter
4 dl / 2 cups milk
50 g / 2 tbsp yeast
1 egg
1 dl / ½ cup sugar
1 pinch of salt

1 pinch of ammonium carbonate (can substitute with baking powder, although result may not be as airy)
14–16 dl / 7–8 cups white all-purpose flour

Topping:
1 dl / ½ cup melted butter
1 dl / ½ cup of granulated sugar
1 dl / ½ cup powdered sugar
2 tbsp vanilla sugar

Melt the butter in a saucepan and add the milk. Let the liquid become lukewarm. Crumble the yeast in a bowl. Pour the lukewarm liquid on top and stir it so that it dissolves. Add eggs, sugar, salt, ammonium carbonate, and almost all of the flour. Save some flour for the kneading. Work the dough until it is smooth and even. It should be quite sticky, but should hold together and not stick to the walls of the bowl. Do not add a lot of extra flour that may make the kringles too dry. Cover the dough and let it rise for 30 minutes. Afterwards, knead it on a floured table. Add the rest of the flour if needed. Set the oven to 225 C / 440 F degrees. Divide the dough into 30 equal parts. Roll the pieces out into lengths of 25–30 cm / 10–12 in. Shape the lengths into kringles or something resembling a pretzel. You could also make round buns if you prefer. Place them on parchment paper and let them rise for an additional 30 minutes. Bake in the middle of the oven for 8 to 10 minutes. Let the kringles cool somewhat. Melt the butter and brush the kringles with it. Mix sugar, powdered sugar, and vanilla sugar and sift a generous amount over the kringles. (See picture p. 103.)

> ## Tip!
> If you are planning to freeze the kringles, do not garnish until they are thawed.

WHEAT LOAVES WITH PISTACHIO FILLING

If you like sweet wheat loaves you have to try this recipe. Since the yeast is dissolved in cold milk, this particular dough provides a crisp croissant-like and moist wheat bread.

4 LOAVES
....

Dough:
50 g / 2 tbsp yeast
5 dl / 2 ½ cups cold milk
3 dl / 1 ½ cups sugar
1 tsp salt
2 tsp ground cardamom
14–16 dl / 7–8 cups white all-purpose flour
200 g / 1 ⅓ sticks butter

Pistachio paste:
1 dl / ½ cup sweet almonds
2 dl / 1 cup shelled unsalted pistachios

2 dl / 1 cup powdered sugar
1 tbsp water
A few drops green food coloring

Pistachio filling:
200 g / 7 oz pistachio paste
200 g / 1 ⅓ sticks butter (room
    temperature)
1 ½ dl / ⅓ cup brown sugar
100 g / 3.5 oz pistachio nuts

Garnish:
1 egg
Granulated sugar

Crumble the yeast in a bowl and whisk it with the cold milk. Add sugar, salt, and cardamom. Stir in 14 dl / 7 cups of flour and work the dough until smooth and even. Divide the butter into smaller pieces and work it into the dough, adding some extra flour if needed. Let it rise for about an hour.

Scald and shell the almonds. Finely grind the nuts in a nut grinder or a food processor. Add powdered sugar, water, and food coloring. Mix until the mass is soft and smooth. Shape the paste into a roll. Roughly grate 200g / 7 oz of the pistachio paste and mix it with butter, brown sugar, and the chopped nuts. (You may freeze the remaining pistachio paste.)

Roll out four sheets of dough of about 25x45 cm / 10x18 in. Cover the dough sheets with the pistachio filling. After they are completely covered, roll the dough up like a roll cake. Cut X-shaped gashes in the tops of the loaves and pull the corners up and out. This will create decorative little peaks on the top of your bread. Set the oven to 200 C / 390 F degrees. Let the loaves rise for 30 minutes. Brush with beaten egg and sprinkle the granulated sugar on top. Bake for about 25 minutes. (See picture on p. 103.)

ORANGE AND CHOCOLATE SCONES
WITH HAZELNUTS

ABOUT 20 SCONES

10 dl / 5 cups extra fine white
   all-purpose flour

½ tsp salt

225 g / 2 sticks butter (room temperature)

Grated zest and juice of 1 orange

1 tsp vanilla sugar

1 dl / ½ cup sugar

4 dl / 2 cups light sour cream

100 g / 3.5 oz dark chocolate (70
   percent)

1 egg for brushing

50 g / 1.7 oz hazelnuts

Mix flour and salt and stir it in with the butter. Add orange zest and juice, vanilla sugar, and sugar. Add sour cream and chopped chocolate. Let the dough sit for about 30 minutes. Set the oven to 225 C / 440 F degrees. Flatten the dough on a lightly floured table and press the scone shapes out by using a cookie cutter. Place them in paper cups and brush with the beaten egg. Roughly chop the hazelnuts and sprinkle them on top. Bake for 12 to 15 minutes.

CLASSIC SCONES

Like English scones, serve them as a snack or invite some friends over for tea some afternoon. The tasty chocolate cream on the next page and the passion fruit curd on page 110 are great with these.

ABOUT 20 SCONES

About 9 dl / 4 ½ cups white
   all-purpose flour
½ tsp salt
1 tbsp baking powder
1 dl / ½ cup sugar
200 g / 1 ⅓ sticks refrigerated butter
2–3 dl / 1–1 ½ cups light buttermilk
1 egg
½ dl / ¼ cup raw cane sugar

Cream cheese crème with a
   taste of lime:
Grated zest of 1–2 limes
2 tbsp lime juice
200 g / 7 oz cream cheese (for
   instance, Philadelphia cream
   cheese)
2 tbsp powdered sugar

Set the oven to 225 C / 440 F degrees. Blend flour, salt, baking powder, and sugar. Dice the butter and work it in with the dry blend. Bind the dough by adding the buttermilk and work it into a ball. Add more flour if the dough is sticky. Let the dough rest in the fridge for about an hour. Put the dough on a floured table and flatten it so that it's about 3 mm / ¹⁄₁₀ of an inch thick. Cut scones with the help of a glass or cookie cutter. Place the scones on a baking sheet lined with parchment paper. Beat the egg and brush the scones with it. Finally, sprinkle some raw cane sugar on top. Bake for 12 to 15 minutes, until they have a nice color.

   Mix all of the ingredients for the cream cheese crème into a smooth cream. Serve the cream cheese crème as a delicious spread for your scones.

CHOCOLATE CREAM
For cakes, scones, toasted bread, or brioche

1 SMALL JAR

200 g / 7 oz dark chocolate (70 percent)

1 vanilla bean

½ dl / ¼ cup milk

1 ½ dl / ⅓ cup heavy whipping cream

2 tbsp sugar

75 g / 5 tbsp refrigerated butter

Finely chop the chocolate by hand or in a mixer. Cut the vanilla bean open and scrape out the seeds. Bring milk, cream, sugar, vanilla seeds, and the vanilla bean to a boil. Let it simmer for 2–3 minutes while stirring. Remove the vanilla bean and throw it out. Slowly pour the warm liquid over the chopped chocolate. Stir with small movements in the middle of the bowl while the chocolate is melting. Dice the butter. Add the pieces of butter when the chocolate is completely melted and the mass is smooth and creamy. Whisk everything vigorously for one minute. Pour the cream into a jar or a small bowl and let it stabilize at room temperature. Keep it in the fridge. It will keep for about a week.

PASSION FRUIT CURD
For cakes, scones, toasted bread, or brioche

1 JAR
. . . . .

8–10 small passion fruits or 4 large

1 lemon (optional)

2 eggs

2 dl / 1 cup raw cane sugar

100 g / 7 tbsp refrigerated butter

> ### Tip!
> If you prefer a lemon curd you can use 1 dl / ½ cup of lemon juice (2 large lemons) instead of the passion fruits. The curd may also be mixed with heavy whipping cream and used as a filling in tarts or roll cakes.

Slice open the fruits and scoop out the meat. Warm the fruit meat in a frying pan; however, it should not boil. Stir while you warm it for about 3 to 4 minutes; the seeds should let go of the juice and fruit meat. If needed you may add a couple of teaspoons of water. Squeeze all the juice from the cores by using a strainer and a spoon. If you don't get the full 1 dl / ½ cup of juice you may supplement with freshly squeezed lemon juice.

Whisk the eggs and sugar until fluffy. Add the fruit juice. Pour the whole batter into a saucepan and warm up on low heat (be careful with the heat so that the batter doesn't stiffen). Keep stirring for a couple of minutes until the cream has become thick and airy. Remove the saucepan from the stove. Add the butter in pieces while stirring. Let it cool, first in room temperature and then in the fridge.

BLUEBERRY SCONES

Just like any other baking powder–based bread or pastry, these wonder-ful scones taste the best when they are still warm.

24 SCONES

8 dl / 4 cups white all-purpose flour
1 tbsp baking powder
1 tsp salt
1 dl / ½ cup sugar

2 eggs
2 ½ dl / 1 ¼ cups buttermilk
1 dl / ½ cup canola oil
250 g / 9 oz frozen or fresh blueberries

Set the oven to 225 C / 440 F degrees. Mix all of the dry ingredients in a bowl. Whisk the eggs and buttermilk together in a bowl of their own. Stir the egg mixture and the canola oil in with the dry ingredients. Lastly, add the blueberries. Be careful when you stir so that you do not smash the berries. A few rounds with the ladle should be sufficient. Scoop the batter into butte-red paper cups, silicon shapes, or muffin pans. Bake for 12 to 15 minutes.

LEMON TWISTS

These lemon- and vanilla-scented buns could make any person cheerful.
Buns, twists, loaves, braids, or wreaths: This wheat dough may be prepa-
red an infinite number of ways.

ABOUT 40 BUNS

Dough:
150 g / 1 ¼ sticks butter
5 dl / 2 ½ cups milk
50 g / 2 tbsp yeast
1 dl / ½ cup white syrup
½ tsp salt
14–15 dl / 7–7 ½ cups white
    all-purpose flour

Filling:
Grated zest and juice of 1 lemon
1 tbsp vanilla sugar
150 g / 1 ¼ sticks butter (room
    temperature)

Brushing:
1 egg
3 tbsp granulated sugar

Melt the butter in a saucepan. Add the milk and keep the liquid on the stove until it turns lukewarm. Crumble the yeast in a bowl and stir in the lukewarm liquid and syrup so that it dissolves. Add salt and flour. Save about 2 dl / 1 cup of the flour for the kneading later on.

Work the dough until it feels smooth. Let it rise for an hour. Place the dough on a floured table and knead it. Divide the dough in two and roll the two parts out into rectangles of about 30x40 cm / 12x16 in.

Mix lemon zest and juice with the vanilla sugar and butter. Cover the two dough rectangles with the lemon cream. Fold the rectangles over to their middles and flatten. Cut 20 equal-size parts out of each rectangle, across. Cut a slit in every piece so that they look like a pair of pants. Twist the legs separately and then tie them together into a careless knot. Place on a baking sheet lined with parchment paper. Set the oven to 225 C / 440 F degrees. Let the twists rise for 30 minutes. Brush them with beaten egg and sprinkle the granulated sugar on top. Bake in the middle of the oven for about 8 minutes.

Tip!

You may add a little extra lemon zest to the granulated sugar to enhance the lemon taste. If you want to make the buns more luxurious you can melt about 100 g / 3.5 oz of white chocolate and drizzle over the buns once they have cooled. Let the chocolate stiffen. It tastes fantastic!

PANETTONE WITH LIMONCELLO

Panettone—the stately New Year's cake from Italy—is baked in a variety of flavors with many different kinds of creams and fillings. The cake is often described as being a cross between a wheat bun and a sugar cake. It is sold, despite the fact that it is a holiday cake, year round. If you celebrate New Year's Eve in Italy, Panettone and Spumante, or champagne, is the preferred choice when the clock strikes midnight.

ABOUT 10 SLICES

- 1 dl / ½ cup yellow raisins
- 100 g / 3.5 oz candied oranges or ginger
- 1 dl / ½ cup lemon liqueur, like Limoncello
- 2 dl / 1 cup milk, 2 percent
- 25 g / 1 ¼ tbsp yeast for sweet dough
- 1 tbsp honey
- 1 dl / ½ cup sugar
- 6–7 dl / 3–3 ½ cups white all-purpose flour
- 150 g / 1 ¼ sticks butter
- 1 tbsp vanilla sugar
- 3 egg yolks
- ½ tsp salt
- Grated zest of 1 lemon
- Butter for the pan and brushing the buns

Soak the raisins and candied orange or ginger in the liqueur for about two hours. Warm the milk so that it's lukewarm. Crumble the yeast in a bowl and dissolve it in the warm milk. Add the honey, half of the sugar, and most of the flour. Cover the bowl and let it rise for about an hour.

Melt the butter. Stir in the rest of the sugar, vanilla sugar, egg yolks, liqueur, raisins, and the candied orange or ginger. Mix well. Put the dough on a table, covered with a layer of flour, and work in the rest of the flour and the lemon zest. Shape the dough into a large ball. Butter a large, tall, and round soufflé dish that holds about 1 ½ liter / 7 ½ cups. Place the dough in the dish and let it rise for 30 minutes. Set the oven to 250 C / 480 F degrees. Brush the dough with melted butter. Bake at the bottom of the oven for 10 minutes. Then, lower the temperature to 150 C / 300 F degrees and bake for an additional 45 to 50 minutes. Cover the cake with aluminum foil if it is turning too dark. Brush with butter when you have 20 minutes of the baking time left. Remove the cake and let it cool for a while before you remove it from the dish, and let it finish cooling on a grid.

CRISPY CARDAMOM WHEAT
BREAD IN SQUARES

It may very well be that this is not the world's quickest made or most beautiful wheat bread; however, I dare to declare it the world's best tasting. Thanks to the long time given to raising the dough, the cake is fluffy while also having a fresh taste of both cardamom and lemon. The crispy caramel-like cinnamon mixture gives the cake a crunchy topping. Delicious!

ABOUT 30 SQUARES

Wheat bread:
100 g / 7 tbsp butter
4 dl / 2 cups milk
25 g / 0.9 oz yeast
12–13 dl / 6–6 ½ cups white
   all-purpose flour
1 dl / ½ cup sugar
½ tsp salt

2 tsp ground cardamom
Grated zest of 1 lemon

Cinnamon topping:
150 g / 1 ¼ stick butter (room
   temperature)
200 g / 7 oz light muscovado sugar
   (or light brown sugar)
1–2 tbsp cinnamon

Melt the butter in a saucepan. Add the milk and heat until the liquid is lukewarm. Sprinkle the yeast in a bowl. Pour in the lukewarm liquid and stir to dissolve the yeast. Add flour, sugar, salt, cardamom, and lemon zest. Mix and knead the dough well; it should be quite loose but still not stick to the surface. Let the dough rise at room temperature for two hours.

Mix the soft butter with the muscovado sugar and cinnamon. Line a baking pan, about 30x40 cm / 12x16 in., with parchment paper. Roll out the dough and place it on the pan. Spread the dough out and flatten it. Cover it with the cinnamon topping. Set the oven to 175 C / 350 F degrees. Let it rise for an additional 30 minutes. Bake the cake for 15 to 20 minutes.

BUTTER CAKE WITH VANILLA CREAM
AND ALMOND PASTE

When I was a child, I always thought that my grandmother's fantastic butter cake was named after Butter, one of the seven dwarves from the Swedish Snow White tale. This is clearly not the case; rather, the cake's name is from the English and German word "butter." This is one of the best holiday cakes out there.

8–10 SLICES
. . . .

Dough:
5 dl / 2 ½ cups white all-purpose flour
½ dl / ¼ cup sugar
125 g / 1 stick butter
25 g / 1 ¼ tbsp yeast for sweet dough
1 dl / ½ cup cream
½ g (1 packet) / ⅓–½ of saffron
   or 2 tsp cardamom
1 egg

Vanilla filling:
1 egg
1 yolk
3 tbsp sugar

1 tbsp white all-purpose flour
⅓ dl / ⅙ cup cream
2 dl / 1 cup milk
1 tbsp vanilla sugar

Cinnamon and almond filling:
200 g / 7 oz almond paste
75 g / 5 tbsp butter
4 tbsp sugar
1 tbsp cinnamon
½ dl / ¼ cup raisins
1 egg

Frosting:
1 dl / ½ cup powdered sugar
1 tbsp water

Mix flour and sugar. Add spoonfuls of butter and stir into a chunky mass. Crumble the yeast in a bowl. Warm cream and saffron or cardamom until it's lukewarm. Pour the liquid over the yeast and stir to dissolve it. Work the yeast liquid in with the flour blend. Lastly, add the egg and work the dough until smooth and even. Let it rise for an hour.

Whisk eggs, yolk, and sugar in a saucepan. Add flour while you are whisking. Add cream and milk. Continue whisking the simmering mixture until it thickens. Remove the saucepan from the stove. Add the vanilla sugar. Let it cool, stirring now and then.

Grate the almond paste and mix it with butter, sugar, and cinnamon.

Set the oven to 200 C / 390 F degrees. Butter a springform, about 24 cm / 9 in. in diameter. Cut about ⅓ of the dough away and set aside for later. Roll the dough out into a round cake a little bit larger than the springform. Place the dough cake in the form and push the edges up 2–3 cm / 1 in. Cover the dough with the vanilla cream. Roll out the other dough piece to a rectangle of about 20x30 cm / 8x12 in. Cover it with the cinnamon filling and sprinkle raisins on top. Roll the rectangle together like a roll cake, starting from the short end. Slice into eight buns. Place the buns on top of the vanilla cream. Let the cake rise for 30 minutes. Brush with the beaten egg and bake in the middle of the oven for about 30 minutes. Mix powdered sugar and water. Drizzle the frosting over the cake when it has cooled.

INDEX

GINGERBREAD HOUSE IN 6 PIECES
+ Use your own imagination for windows and doors

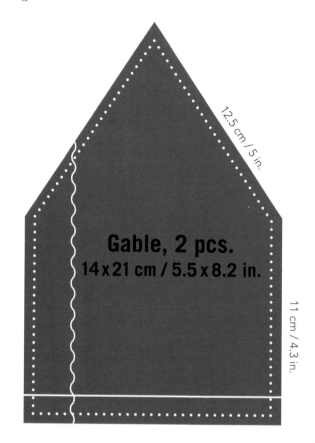

Roof, two pcs.
20 x 14 cm / 7.8 x 5.5 in.

12.5 cm / 5 in.

Gable, 2 pcs.
14 x 21 cm / 5.5 x 8.2 in.

11 cm / 4.3 in.

Front+Back, 2 pcs.
11 x 18 cm / 4.3 x 7.1 in.

Scale 1:2